Credits

WRITING
JEFFREY BARBER, SHANNON KALVAR, LYSLE KAPP, SAM WITT

ORIGINAL CAMPAIGN CREATION AND DEVELOPMENT
GREG BENAGE

LEAD DEVELOPER
ROB VAUGHN

MANAGING DEVELOPER
GREG BENAGE

COVER ILLUSTRATION
J. P. TARGETE

INTERIOR ILLUSTRATIONS
DAVID GRIFFITH, CONSTANTINOS KONIOTIS, ANNETH LAGAMO, TIERAN NORDSTRAND, HIAN RODRIGUEZ

GRAPHIC DESIGN
BRIAN SCHOMBURG

COPY EDITING
GREG BENAGE, ROB VAUGHN

CONTENT EDITING, LAYOUT, AND ART DIRECTION
ROB VAUGHN

PUBLISHER
CHRISTIAN T. PETERSEN

FANTASY FLIGHT GAMES
1975 County Rd. B2 #1
Roseville, MN 55113
www.fantasyflightgames.com

Contents

Introduction	3
Chapter One: Demons of the Aruun	4
Crawler	4
Dark Walker	5
Flesh-Clad Spirit	6
Grenghost	7
Vine Beast	8
Husbanded Creature	9
Noble Demon	10
Reality Sink	12
Tuk	14
Chapter Two: Creatures of Eredane	15
Bitterwind	15
Blight Ogre	16
Carrion Stag	18
Degenerate Darghuul	19
Earthback	20
Forsaken	21
Ogre Damen	23
Otherworlders	25
The Berserk	25
The Herald	26
The Mender	26
The Warden	27
Puppeteer	28
Razor	29
Sundered Beast	31
Gloom Hound	31
Splinter Steed	33
Chapter Three: Spirits and Allies	34
Craft Current	34
Guardian Grove	35
Vigil Vine	35
Bulwark Hedge	35
Sentinel Tree	36
Guardian Spirit	37
Heepa-Heepa	38
Highland Imp	39
Leaper	40
Lore Pool	41
Seedra	42
Vassal Spirit	43
Chapter Four: Animals of Eredane	44
Boro	44
Grass Cat	45
Ort	45
Plains Leopard	46
Sea Dragon	47
Chapter Five: Agents of Shadow	48
Ceelian/Asale	48
Darshod of the Dead Mother Tribe	49
Gorgathan of the Mother of Bone Tribe	51
Grial the Fey Killer	52
Shealgruf One-Arm	53
Purlan Marrick	54
Zebrim the Slaver	55
Sample Legates	
Lesser Legate	57
Soldier Legate	57
Veteran Soldier Legate	57
Temple Legate	57
Sample Orcs	
Orc Recruit	58
Orc Scout	59
Orc Elite	59
Orc Marauder	59
Oruk Shock Troop	59
Oruk Commander	59
Appendix 1: D&D 3.5 Updated	**60**
Midnight Spell List	
Appendix 2: Errata for MIDNIGHT	**62**
and MIDNIGHT: Against the Shadow	

Introduction

Minions of the Shadow

From the bitter cold of the peaks of the Highhorn Mountains to the burning wastes of the White Desert, creatures both fell and mysterious prey on the unwary. Demons and bodiless spirits lurk in the Aruun Jungle, waiting for their day of freedom. Unnamed, alien beings lie dormant beneath the Kaladrun Mountaints, dreaming of impossible worlds. Though these beasts and monsters are seemingly separate, those who fight Izrador know the truth: They all, whether knowingly or not, serve the purposes of the Shadow.

Chapter One: Demons of the Aruun presents the creatures of that dark jungle hinted at in the MIDNIGHT core book. These beings are both physical and incorporeal, beastial and intelligent. Their greatest weapons are deception and fear, and they have the power to turn the plants, animals, and even children of the forest dwellers against them.

Chapter Two: Creatures of Eredane addresses the wider array of foes that adventurers are likely to encounter throughout the lands controlled by Izrador's minions. Some are merely hunters, other are prize servants of the dark lord himself.

Chapter Three: Spirits and Allies offers a small glimmer of hope. The magical beasts and outsiders here are the long-time friends of the people of Aryth, though many can just as easily be used by Izrador and his legates.

Chapter Four: Animals of Eredane takes a look at the normal creatures of MIDNIGHT's ecosystems. Some are used for food, war, and hunting, while others are dangerous in their own right and left alone by all but the most desperate or most foolish.

Chapter Five: Agents of Shadow provides statistics and detailed backgrounds for major players among Izrador's forces. Some are legendary, others are secretive and unassuming, but all are extremely dangerous.

We hope you enjoy this look into the dangers of MIDNIGHT. Visit our web site at http://www.fantasyflightgames.com/midnight.html for web supplements and more MIDNIGHT news.

The Open Game License

Minions of the Shadow is published under the terms of the Open Game License and d20 System Trademark License. The OGL allows us to use the d20 System core rules and to publish gaming material derived from those rules.

In fact, material that is strictly rules related is Open Content. You can use this material in your own works, as long as you follow the conditions of the Open Game License. You can copy the material to your website or even put it in a book that you publish and sell.

Not everything in this book is Open Content, however. The names of creatures and characters are designated as Open Content, as are any game statistics, mechanics, and rules derived from the d20 SRD. The descriptions of the creatures and the characters' backgrounds are are closed content and cannot be republished, copied, or distributed without the consent of Fantasy Flight Games.

All illustrations, pictures, and diagrams in this book are Product Identity and the property of Fantasy Flight Games, © 2003.

The Open Game License is printed in its entirety at the end of this book. For further information, please visit the Open Gaming Foundation website at www.opengamingfoundation.org.

Chapter One

Demons of the Aruun

Crawler

Medium Outsider
Hit Dice: 8d8+16 (52 hp)
Initiative: +2
Speed: 30 ft. (6 squares), climb 15 ft.
AC: 18 (+2 Dex, +6 natural), touch 12, flat-footed 16
Base Attack/Grapple: +8/+12
Attack: 2 claws +12 melee (1d8+4)
Full Attack: 2 claws +12 melee (1d8+4), bite +7 melee (1d6+2)
Face/Reach: 5 ft./5 ft.
Special Attacks: Baffling howl, improved grab
Special Qualities: Fast healing 3, scent
Saves: Fort +8, Ref +8, Will +7
Abilities: Str 18, Dex 15, Con 14, Int 5, Wis 12, Cha 7
Skills: Climb +17, Jump +18, Listen +14, Spot +14, Survival +12, Tumble +13
Feats: Alertness, Power Attack, Track
Environment: Aruun Jungle
Organization: Solitary, pair, or pack (3–9)
Challenge Rating: 6
Treasure: None
Alignment: Always neutral evil
Advancement: 9–16 HD (Medium); 17–24 (Large)

Breaking forth from the thick undergrowth is a pack of feral, ape-like creatures. They race toward you, propelled by powerful forearms, as their terrifying cries echo through the surrounding trees.

Crawlers are cunning, ape-like creatures that roam the Aruun in packs. Thick, ashen hair covers their entire body save for their bony faces and razor-sharp claws. Their eyes are often obsidian or a deep red in color. The greatest of these monstrous demons can reach nearly nine feet tall and top 900 pounds.

Despite their great strength and deadly claws, what survivors recall most vividly from their encounters with crawlers are the horrific sounds the creatures make. Crawlers communicate through a series of hyena-like cackles and piercing shrieks that chill the bones of those who hear them. More than one unfortunate victim has succumbed to the crawler's fiendish cries and become hopelessly lost within the jungles of southern Erethor. Any Danisil guide who bears the scars of adulthood will insist that those who travel with him are properly prepared to deal with these fiends.

Crawlers are highly social creatures. Although the creatures are far less intelligent than the average humanoid, crawler packs display remarkable cunning and coordination during the hunt. Many scholars believe that crawlers are descended from fiendish servitors and lesser demons who accompanied their masters to Aryth in ancient times. In the confusion of the Sundering, these ancestors escaped their taskmasters and slavers, fleeing to the thick growth of the jungles and banding together for protection. Eventually, as they adapted to jungle life, growing in number and strength, the hunted became the hunters.

In addition to their own language, those crawlers with higher Intelligence scores also speak the Black Tongue.

Combat

Crawlers are aggressive pack hunters. One or more of their number often scout ahead searching for suitable prey. The scouts try to disorient their victims or otherwise lure their prey into secluded areas where the rest of the pack lies in wait.

Baffling Howl (Ex): As a standard action, a crawler can emit a loud howl that disorients its opponents. Those within 30 ft. of a howling crawler must make a

DC 16 Will save or suffer the effects of a *confusion* spell for 2d4 rounds (caster level 8, save DC is Constitution-based). If another crawler is using its baffling howl, the effect of each becomes more potent. For each crawler within 30 ft. that is using its baffling cry, the DC for the requisite Will save increases by +1 and the duration of the effect increases by one additional round.

Improved Grab (Ex): To use this ability, the crawler must hit with both of its claw attacks. It can then attempt to start a grapple as a free action without provoking an attack of opportunity. If it wins the grapple check, it establishes a hold and can rake.

Rake (Ex): Attack bonus +8 melee, damage 1d6+2.

Fast Healing (Ex): A crawler regains lost hit points at a rate of 3 per round. Fast healing does not restore hit points lost from starvation, thirst, or suffocation, and it does not allow the crawler to regrow or reattach lost body parts.

Skills: Crawlers receive a +8 racial bonus on Climb and Jump checks.

Dark Walker

Medium Outsider (Incorporeal)
Hit Dice: 12d8+12 (66 hp)
Initiative: +3
Speed: 30 ft. (6 squares), fly 15 ft. (poor)
AC: 13 (+3 Dex), touch 13, flat-footed 10
Base Attack/Grapple: +12/+12
Attack: Claw +12 melee (1d8)
Full Attack: 2 claws +12 melee (1d8)
Face/Reach: 5 ft./5 ft.
Special Attacks: Spell-like abilities
Special Qualities: Incorporeal, regeneration 1, mind ride, shadow form, sunlight vulnerability
Saves: Fort +9, Ref +11, Will +8
Abilities: Str 10, Dex 16, Con 13, Int 10, Wis 11, Cha 21
Skills: Bluff +20, Handle Animal +20, Hide +15, Knowledge (arcane) +15, Listen +15, Move Silently +18, Spellcraft +15, Spot +15
Feats: Blind-fight, Dodge, Improved Initiative, Mobility, Spring Attack
Environment: Aruun Jungle
Organization: Solitary
Challenge Rating: 10
Treasure: None
Alignment: Usually neutral evil
Advancement: 13–24 HD (Medium); 25–36 (Large)

A menacing, shadowy humanoid form lunges toward you. Though not quite corporeal, its fierce claws appear substantial enough to tear a man to shreds.

Dark walkers are manifestations of demons trapped within the ruins of Ibon-sul. Although they are loathe to serve any master, these demons have made dark pacts with Izrador in exchange for the promise of freedom once his powers are fully restored.

The Shadow knows that the dark walkers desire the freedom to leave the ruins, but he also knows that his powers are not absolute and that a group of powerful demons could do much to hinder his carefully constructed plans. To that end, the Shadow has provided these demons with new bodies constructed of shadow to contain their spirits. These shadow forms allow the demons to leave the ruins, unhindered by the magical wards that keep their physical bodies in check. In exchange, the demons are charged with hunting down Danisil and carrying out the Dark One's will.

However, these forms are as illusory as most of Izrador's promises, and are only partially real. Many dark walkers have yet to realize that the Shadow's "gift" is largely a false one and would be enraged should they ever learn the truth.

In addition to their own language, those dark walkers with high Intelligence scores also speak Black Tongue, Jungle Mouth, or Orcish.

Combat

Dark walkers rely on deception and ambush, using their mind ride ability to locate and track prey. If a dark walker's illusory nature is discovered or opponents demonstrate substantial fighting prowess, a dark walker often flees into the jungle to plot anew.

Regeneration (Su): A dark walker's shadowy body constantly replenishes itself. The only thing that deals normal damage to dark walkers is sunlight (which inflicts 1d8 points of damage per round) and spells like *searing light, sunbeam,* and *sunburst*, which inflict damage on the dark walker as if it were undead.

Mind Ride (Su): A dark walker can attempt to ride the mind of any living creature within 60 ft. The target must make a DC 21 Will save; failure means that the dark walker can now see, hear, smell, and feel everything that the ridden creature experiences. The creature has no idea that it was attacked, or that the dark walker is riding its mind. The dark walker's shadow form dissipates while he is riding a mind, and when the dark walker disengages from its target, its body reforms at the spot it last was when it attacked the mind. A dark walker cannot leap from mind to mind without first reforming its body. A target that succeeds at the save realizes that something attacked its mind, and is immune to the dark walker's mind ride ability for one day. The save DC is Charisma-based.

Shadow Form (Su): The dark walker's body is composed of quasi-real shadow and is partially illusory. A dark walker is able to shape its form to appear much stronger and deadly than it truly is. The dark walker has the following altered statistics as long as an opponent has yet to disbelieve the dark walker's illusory appearance: 114 hp; AC 21 (+3 Dex, +8 natural); Base Atk +12; Grp +16; Atks +16 melee (2d6+4, 2 claws); Space/Reach 5 ft./10 ft.; SA rend (if hits with both claws, may rend for 4d6+6); SQ blur (20% miss chance); Str 18, Con 21.

All those who interact with the dark walker can make a DC 21 Will save to recognize its shadowy nature. Those who succeed see the dark walker as a transparent image superimposed on a vague, shadowy form, and interact with the dark walker as normal. Once a creature succeeds, it is immune to the illusory nature of the dark walker for 24 hours.

A dark walker's quasi-real shadow form allows it to move through solid objects, although each square of solid objects counts as 4 squares for movement purposes.

Spell-like Abilities: 3/day—*shadow conjuration* (DC 19), *shadow evocation* (DC 20). Caster level 12. Save DC is Charisma-based.

Sunlight Vulnerability (Ex): When exposed to natural sunlight, dark walkers suffer 1d8 points of damage per round and are considered nauseated. A *daylight* spell hedges out a dark walker unless it makes a Fort save (DC varies by caster); even if it succeeds, it is considered sickened as long as it is within the spell's radius.

Flesh—Clad Spirit

Medium Outsider
Hit Dice: 5d8+5 (27)
Initiative: +3
Speed: 30 ft. (6 squares), fly 10 ft.
AC: 16 (+3 Dex, +3 natural), touch 13, flat-footed 13
Base Attack/Grapple: +5/+5
Attack: Flensing caress +8 melee touch attack (2d4)
Full Attack: Flensing caress +8 melee touch attack (2d4)
Space/Reach: 5 ft./5 ft.
Special Attacks: Flensing caress
Special Qualities: Blindsight 60 ft., unstable incorporeal form
Saves: Fort +5, Ref +7, Will +4
Abilities: Str 10, Dex 16, Con 13, Int 15, Wis 11, Cha 11
Skills: Disguise +8, Escape Artist +11, Hide +11, Listen +8, Move Silently +11, Search +10, Tumble +11, Spot +8
Feats: Combat Expertise, Weapon Finesse (flensing caress)
Environment: Any
Organization: Solitary, pair, or pack (4–6)
Challenge Rating: 4
Treasure: Standard
Alignment: Always evil
Advancement: 6–10 HD (Large); 11–15 HD (Huge)

A foul and rotting hand suddenly bursts from the shadows, glittering talons clawing through the air to rip the flesh from your bones.

Flesh-clad spirits are terrifying predators, first uncovered by a lost expedition into the Aruun. They have since spread throughout all of Aryth in their various guises, however, and now wander the earth in search of warm, bleeding flesh in which to wrap their incorporeal bodies. While they can, and often do, borrow the flesh of beasts, their bodily forms overall mimic the humanoid form of men and elves. While most of these dreadful creatures are roughly man-sized, the canniest and most dangerous demons can grow to horrible sizes as they accrete greater and greater layers of flesh around their wispy cores. All flesh-clad spirits, regardless of their size, are difficult to mistake for normal, living beings. The layers of flesh that surround them are often of various races and shapes, and loose flaps of skin ooze bodily fluids continously.

The largest and oldest flesh-clad spirits hide themselves deep within the Aruun, where they gather skin and meat brought to them by others of their kind. Legends amongst the Danisil whisper of the Broken King, a colossal flesh-clad spirit that writhes in constant agony as its lesser brethren attempt to bring it back to the world of men. Though Izrador holds little stock in such tales, more than a few of his captains watch the Aruun warily, and their troops often hunt these creatures in an attempt to forestall any plans they may have.

Combat

Flesh-clad spirits are insatiable hunters that go to great lengths to kill any living creatures who cross their path. They generally attempt to use stealth to their advantage, lying in wait along well-traveled roads or near resting areas where prey is plentiful and often weary. In areas where hiding is difficult and cover sparse, a canny spirit may disguise itself with rags and attempt to pass itself off as a wandering vagabond. When the prey drops its guard, the flesh-clad spirit lunges in for the kill, tearing flesh from bone with frightening ease.

Flensing Caress (Su): Flesh-clad spirits, while denied bodies of their own, are gifted with the ability to shred flesh from bone with a mere touch. The rent tissue is immediately absorbed, plastered onto the layers of bloody flesh already surrounding the flesh clad spirit. This attack bypasses all armor, because the tips of the spirit's talons are incorporeal. The flesh-clad spirit heals a number of hit points equal to the damage done. If it succeeds at a critical hit while at full hit points, the flesh-clad spirit absorbs enough flesh to increase its power, immediately advancing one Hit Die and possibly increasing in size.

Unstable Incorporeal Form: A flesh-clad spirit's true body is an incorporeal knot of malice and vile cunning. Such bodies quickly disperse in this world, requiring the flesh-clad spirit to steal others' flesh to survive. Flesh-clad spirits' stolen flesh is constantly dying, however, and the creatures lose 1 hit point per day. Whenever a flesh-clad spirit is reduced to 10 or fewer hit points, it immediately becomes incorporeal. At that point, it can be harmed only by other incorporeal creatures, +1 or better magical weapons, or magic, with a 50% chance to ignore any damage from a corporeal source. It can pass through solid objects at will, and its own attacks pass through armor. While incorporeal, the flesh-clad spirit always moves silently.

However, at the end of any round in which the flesh-clad spirit is incorporeal, it suffers 1 point of damage. When reduced to zero or fewer hit points, the flesh-clad spirit is destroyed, and its demonic essence dissipates harmlessly.

Grenghost

Small Outsider (Incorporeal)
Hit Dice: 2d8 (9 hp)
Initiative: +6
Speed: Fly 40 ft. (good)
AC: 16 (+1 size, +2 Dex, +3 deflection), touch 13, flat-footed 14

Base Attack/Grapple: +2/—
Attack: —
Full Attack: —
Space/Reach: 5 ft./5 ft.
Special Attacks: Plant possession
Special Qualities: Incorporeal, natural invisibility
Saves: Fort +3, Ref +5, Will +5
Abilities: Str —, Dex 15, Con 10, Int 14, Wis 15, Cha 16
Skills: Hide +6, Listen +6, Knowledge (arcana) +6, Knowledge (nature) +6, Knowledge (the planes) +6, Search +6, Spot +6, Survival +6
Feats: Improved Initiative
Environment: Aruun Jungle
Organization: Solitary, pair, or cabal (3–9)
Challenge Rating: 1
Treasure: None
Alignment: Usually neutral evil
Advancement: 3–6 HD (Small); 7–12 (Medium)

The vines before you begin to twine and writhe, forming a serpent-like shape with dangerously snapping tentacles.

Grenghosts are naturally invisible and incorporeal spirits. Should they become visible, they appear as writhing, floating serpents.

These foul spirits dwell deep with the Aruun, shaping vines into parodies of animals and hunting the Danisil or any other creatures foolish enough to enter their domain. More than one cunning legate has sent expeditions into the Aruun to secure the cooperation of a grenghost, as these demons make fine assassins. They can turn a druid's plant charges against their master or transform a rebel's garden into a death trap.

Combat

Grenghosts have no offensive capabilities in their natural forms, but their ability to inhabit plants assures that they are not helpless in a fight.

Form Vine Beast (Su): A grenghost can merge itself with adjacent inanimate plants and animate them as a full-round action, reshaping them into a form that resembles a normal animal. Use the vine beast template for such forms, below. In addition to being limited by the grenghost's Hit Dice, the type of animal formed also depends upon the amount of plant mass in the area. A grenghost can form a vine beast of up to 2 Hit Dice for every five square feet of plant material available. A grenghost cannot reform a vine beast from the plant material of a destroyed vine beast.

Natural Invisibility (Su): This ability is constant, allowing a grenghost to remain invisible at all times. This ability is inherent and not subject to the *invisibility purge* spell.

Vine Beast (Template)

Vine beasts are creatures formed by the possession of inanimate plants by grenghosts. Through sheer force of will, a grenghost can weave a thatch of grass or vines into a formidable fighting form that mimics the natural weapons and fighting abilities of a local beast. The grenghost can cause vines and branches to perform the functions of muscle, tissue, and bone, and cause the plants it possesses to sprout sharp thorns to emulate teeth, claws, or talons.

Creating A Vine Beast Creature

"Vine beast" is a template that can be applied to any animal (referred to hereafter as the base creature) with no more than twice the Hit Dice of the animating grenghost. A vine beast uses all the base creature's statistics and special abilities except as noted here.

Size and Type: The creature's type changes to plant. Size is unchanged, as are most features (base attack bonus, saves, skill points per Hit Die, etc.).

Hit Dice: Change to d8.

Speed: Same as base creature –10 ft. (minimum of 5 ft.)

AC: Base creature's natural armor improves by +5.

Attacks: The vine beast retains all the attacks of the base creature and also gains four tentacle attacks.

Whichever natural weapon (including the four tentacles) has the highest base damage becomes the vine beast's primary attack. If two natural weapons have the same base damage, the one that also delivers a special attack (such as poison) is primary.

Damage: Same as the base creature. Tentacles deal damage depending upon the vine beast's size as indicated below.

Size	Damage
Fine	1
Diminutive	1d2
Tiny	1d3
Small	1d4
Medium	1d6
Large	1d8
Huge	2d6
Gargantuan	2d8
Colossal	4d6

Special Attacks: A vine beast has all the special attacks of the base creature, plus the following special qualities.

Improved Grab (Ex): To use this ability, the vine beast must hit an opponent at least one size category smaller with a tentacle attack. If it gets a hold, it can constrict.

Constrict (Ex): A vine beast deals automatic tentacle damage with a successful grapple check against held opponents that are at least one size category smaller than the vine beast.

Special Qualities: A vine beast loses all the special qualities of the base creature, but gains the following special qualities.

Fast Healing (Su): A vine beast regains lost hit points at a rate of 2 per round. Fast healing allows the vine beast to regrow severed body parts in 3d6 minutes or to reattach them instantly if held to the stump.

Woodland Stride (Ex): A vine beast can move through natural thorns, briars, overgrown areas, and similar terrain at its normal speed without suffering damage or other impairment. However, thorns, briars, and overgrown areas that are enchanted or magically manipulated to impede motion sill affect the vine beast.

Plant Traits (Ex): A vine beast is immune to poison, *sleep*, paralysis, stunning, and polymorphing and is not subject to critical hits or mind-affecting effects (charms, compulsions, phantasms, patterns, and morale effects). Vine beasts have low-light vision. Vine beasts breathe and eat, but do not sleep.

Saves: The vine beast uses the base creature's Fortitude and Reflex saves and the grenghost's Will save.

Abilities: A vine beast uses the Strength, Dexterity, and Constitution scores of the base creature and the Intelligence, Wisdom, and Charisma scores of the grenghost that created it.

Skills: A vine beast uses the skill points of the grenghost or the animal, whichever is greater. Additionally, the vine beast gains a +15 racial bonus on

Hide checks made in tall grass, heavy undergrowth, or other areas of thick foliage.

Feats: A vine beast gains the Multiattack feat

Climate/Terrain: Aruun Jungle

Organization: Solitary, pair, or cabal (3–9)

Challenge Rating: Same as base creature +1

Treasure: None

Alignment: Same as the animating grenghost's

Husbanded Creature (Template)

It grins gleefully, revealing broken and blackened teeth in a mouth too large for its humanoid head. The thing's arms sag with rotting, cancerous flesh, and move in foul, mystic gestures. Worst of all are its eyes, because looking into them, you can see that this hideous creature was once a mortal man.

Husbanded creatures, or simply "husbands," are foul, hateful men who have bartered away any remnants of their purity and humanity in exchange for favors, and ultimately power, from the fiendish mistresses they serve. Once male humanoids, these wretched monsters bear the scars left by the unforgiving, demonic beings that they are so devoted to serving. Their bodies and faces are pocked with ruptures and are distorted and melted, a reflection of the damage done to their minds and spirits. Their seemingly frail forms quake as they try to contain the tainted energies now seeded within them.

Their devotion to their dark mistresses is unrelenting. A husband will stop at nothing short of death to see the will of his mistress manifest. Likewise, should his mistress ever look upon him with disinterest or disfavor, a husband will threaten entire nations, if need be, to restore his standing with her.

When not plying the trades of their dark mistresses or attempting to garner the attention of one, husbands lead rather solitary lives.

Creating A Husbanded Creature

"Husband" is an acquired template that can be added to any male humanoid, giant, or monstrous humanoid (referred to hereafter as the character) with the following requirements: the creature must not have any class levels in druid, the creature must have made contact with a willing mistress (any female outsider with 10 or more Hit Dice), must have learned the appropriate ritual from her, and must be able to cast *alter self, bestow curse,* and *contagion* and be willing to cast them on himself during the ritual. A husband has all the character's statistics and special abilities except as noted here.

Size and Type: The character's type changes to aberration. Do not recalculate base attack bonus, saves,

or skill points. Size is unchanged.

Hit Dice: Adjust all current and future Hit Dice to d8s and apply new Constitution modifier.

AC: A husband has a +5 natural armor bonus or the character's natural armor bonus, whichever is better.

Attack: A husband gains two claw attacks. Claw damage is as follows: Medium—1d6; Large—1d8; Huge—2d6.

Special Attacks: A husband retains the special attacks of the character and gains the following special attack.

Animal Possession (Su): At will as a standard action, a husband can possess any creature with the animal type within 120 ft. This ability is similar to *magic jar*, except that it does not require a receptacle. If the attack succeeds, the husband's body dissolves into a puddle of acrid puss and bile, and his spirit takes over the animal. The husband may stay in the animal indefinitely; if it is killed, the husband's spirit is trapped at the spot that the animal died until it can possess another animal that comes within range. Alternatively, the husband may emerge from the animal willingly; in this case, the animal dies and its body is reshaped into the husband's previous form. This transformation takes one full round to complete, during which time the husband is helpless.

A husband may cast spells as normal while in the animal's form.

A target that resists the animal possession attack

with a successful save is immune to the husband's possession ability for one day. Caster level is equal to the husband's Hit Dice. The save DC is equal to 15 + the husband's spellcasting attribute.

Special Qualities: A husband retains all the special qualities of the character and gains the following special qualities. Husbands retain familiars if they have them, though a good-aligned familiar will not remain with a husband.

Fast Healing (Su): A husband heals 5 points of damage each round.

Bonded (Su): Husbands are bonded, body and soul, to their mistresses. They generally follow their commands with blind obedience and obsessive love, but in case a husband might have a change of heart, they are also placed under a permanent *charm* effect with regard to their mistresses (never allowed a saving throw, caster level 20). Mistresses may communicate with their husbands via a *sending* spell effect at will.

Limited: Husbands may not advance in any character class except the channeler class after acquiring the husbanded template.

Favor of the Mistress (Su): In exchange for their servitude, husbands gain greater magical power from their mistresses. They may cast channeler spells as if they were one level higher, and all channeler spells cost one less spell energy to cast.

Abilities: Increase from the character as follows: Str +4, Con +8, Dex –2, +8 to spellcasting attribute, –4 to remaining two attributes.

Organization: Solitary.

Challenge Rating: Same as the base creature +2.

Treasure: Double standard.

Alignment: Usually chaotic evil. Few neutral creatures are willing to ply the dark trades required by their fiendish mistresses. A husbanded creature is never good.

Advancement: Same as the base creature.

Level Adjustment: Same as the base creature +4.

Sample Erenlander Husband

Medium Aberration Cha7 (Spiritual)
Hit Dice: 7d6+28 (52 hp)
Initiative: +3
Speed: 30 ft. (6 squares)
AC: 14 (–1 Dex, +5 natural), touch 9, flat-footed 14
Base Attack/Grapple: +5/+9
Attack: Claw +9 melee (1d6+4)
Full Attack: 2 Claws +9 melee (1d6+4)
Space/Reach: 5 ft./5 ft.
Special Attacks: Animal possession, , master of two worlds, spells
Special Qualities: Fast healing 5, bonded, limited, favor of the mistress
Saves: Fort +6, Ref +1, Will +11
Abilities: Str 18, Dex 9, Con 18, Int 6, Wis 22, Cha 4
Skills: Bluff +7, Concentration +14, Knowledge (arcana) +8, Knowledge (Aruun) +8, Listen +16, Profession (herbalist) +10, Sense Motive +16, Spellcraft +8, Spot +16
Feats: Magecraft, Spellcasting (lesser conjuration), Spellcasting (greater conjuration), Spellcasting (necromancy), Spellcasting (transmutation), Improved Initiative, Spell Focus (necromancy), Still Spell, Scribe Scroll
Environment: Any
Organization: Solitary
Challenge Rating: 9
Treasure: Double Standard
Alignment: Usually neutral evil
Advancement: By character class

Before you stands a pathetic looking creature. Its eyes are sunken and its skin droops low on the face as if it had been poured over its misshapen skull. Tattered rags cover scarred and ruptured skin that seems to shake and quiver violently.

Barely resembling the man it once was, this Erenlander husband has devoted its life to furthering the goals of a succubus it encountered deep in the Aruun jungle.

Combat

Animal Possession (Su): Save DC 21.

Spells Known (13 points of spell energy/day; DC 16 + spell level): 0—*arcane mark, create water, detect magic, know direction, mage hand, open/close, prestidigitation, ray of frost, resistance;* 1st—*cause fear*, mage armor, magic weapon, obscuring mist, ray of enfeeblement*;* 2nd—*acid arrow, alter self, blindness/deafness*, cure moderate wounds, false life, ghoul touch*, scare*, summon swarm;* 3rd—*gaseous form, slow, stinking cloud, summon monster III, tongues, water breathing;* 4th—*bestow curse*, black tentacles, contagion*, polymporph.*

* Necromany spell: DC 17 + spell level.

Rituals: polymorph, summon monster III, tongues

Possessions: greater spell talisman (necromancy), spell talisman (*acid arrow*), 10 scrolls with conjuration, necromancy, or transmutation spells.

Noble Demon

Huge Outsider
Hit Dice: 20d8+180 (270 hp)
Initiative: +3
Speed: 40 ft. (8 squares); fly 80 (poor)
AC: 29 (–2 size, +3 Dex, +18 natural), touch 11, flat-footed 26
Base Attack/Grapple: +20/+41
Attack: Bite +33 melee (2d8+13)
Full Attack: Bite +33 melee (2d8+13/19–20/x2), 4

vines +31 melee (1d8+7), 2 claws +31 melee (1d8+7)

Space/Reach: 15 ft./15 ft. (20 ft. with vines)

Special Attacks: Absorbing possession, improved grab, constrict, pounce, distracting speech, spell-like abilities

Special Qualities: Plant-like traits, telepathy 120 ft., blindsight 120 ft., damage reduction 15/mithril and good, true seeing, spell resistance 22

Saves: Fort +21, Ref +15, Will +19

Abilities: Str 37, Dex 16, Con 29, Int 22, Wis 24, Cha 15

Skills: Climb +36, Hide +22, Intimidate +26, Knowledge (arcana) +29, Knowledge (history) +29, Knowledge (planes) +29, Knowledge (religion) +29, Listen +30, Move Silently +26, Search +29, Spot +30, Spellcraft +29, Survival +30

Feats: Awesome Blow, Cleave, Improved Bull Rush, Improved Critical (bite), Multiattack, Power Attack, Quicken Spell-like Ability (animate plants)

Environment: Ruins of Ibon-sul

Organization: Solitary

Challenge Rating: 17

Treasure: Standard

Alignment: Usually neutral evil

Advancement: 21–40 HD (Huge); 41–60 (Gargantuan)

Emerging from the over-grown rubble is a powerful creature that looks as though it is the amalgamation of numerous varieties of plants and animals. Its leonine body supports a large humanoid head surrounded by a main of slithering vines. Its sinewy legs, pocked by thick reptilian scales, end in sharp claws, while massive feathered wings sprout from its shoulders.

Noble demons are horrific monstrosities that haunt the ruins of Ibon-sul. They are restless spirits whose bodies bear the remains of the hapless beasts and plants that they have forcefully possessed and absorbed throughout the centuries.

As the legends go, before the Sundering, the clerics of Ibon-sul summoned powerful demons who were bound, studied, and then destroyed. However, the arrogant clerics of Ibon-sul learned that not all creatures were so easy to control. It is said that there were demons summoned that could not be bound. Though the clerics were able to destroy the demons' bodies, they were unable to contain their spirits, and the formless demons constructed new bodies for themselves from the life forms that dwelled in and around the city. None can say for certain if these tales are true, for the city has been long destroyed and those who venture near the ruins are seldom heard from again.

Noble demons speak Infernal, Abyssal, and Celestial; they also have the ability to communicate telepathically with any creature within 120 ft., even plants and animals (as if using the *speak with plants* or *speak with animals* spells).

Combat

Noble demons attack with their deadly bite to make short work of their victims. When facing more than one opponent, a noble demon often seeks to devour its weakest foes while holding the others at bay with its vines or sharp claws.

Absorbing Possession (Su): Once per round, a noble demon can possess another living creature within 400 ft. unless it makes a DC 27 Will save. This ability is similar to the *magic jar* spell, except that it does not require a receptacle and it has an unlimited range once the creature is possessed. The noble demon's form lies dormant but aware while the possession occurs (i.e., it is not helpless). A target that resists the attack with a successful save is immune to the noble demon's possession ability for one day.

A noble demon that remains in possession of a creature for a considerable length of time begins to absorb part of the creature into itself. Every day that a noble demon remains in possession of a creature, the possessed creature must make another DC 27 Will save or suffer 1d4 points of Constitution drain. For each point of Constitution drain dealt in this manner, the noble demon heals 5 hit points, gaining any excess as temporary hit points. The temporary hit points fade at a rate of one hit point every hour. The noble demon's body also gains some cosmetic trait of any creature thus affected . . . a patch of skin may appear on the demon's back, the shape of the creature's face may appear on the demon's belly, feathers may sprout from the demon's legs, etc.

A noble demon may use any of its spell-like abilities while possessing a creature, but doing so ends the possession immediately.

Improved Grab (Ex): To use this ability, the noble demon must hit with its vine attack. If it gets a hold, it can constrict.

Constrict (Ex): A noble demon deals 1d8+7 points of damage with a successful grapple check against a Large or smaller creature.

Pounce (Ex): If a noble demon leaps upon an opponent during the first round of combat, it can make a full attack even if it has already taken a move action.

Distracting Speech (Su): A noble demon can speak with such command and authority that those around it have difficulty concentrating on other things. Concentration checks are required for any complex action performed within 120 ft. of a talking noble demon, such as casting a spell (DC 15 + spell level), developing a plan of attack (DC 20), or making a Knowledge or Heal check (DC 25). A noble demon can use this ability as a free action provided that it is able to speak.

True Seeing (Su): Noble demons have a continuous *true seeing* ability, as per the spell (caster level 20).

Spell-like Abilities (Su): At will—*animate objects, command* (DC 18), *command plants* (DC 21), *detect thoughts* (DC 19), *dispel magic, dominate animal* (DC 20), *tongues*; 3/day—*animate plants, heal, hold monster* (DC 22), *insect plague, suggestion* (DC 20); 1/day—*creeping doom, dominate monster* (DC 26), *greater dispel, mind blank, repulsion* (DC 23). Caster level 20. Save DCs are Wisdom-based.

Plant-like Traits (Ex): Noble demons are partially composed of the absorbed remains of the plants they have possessed. A noble demon is immune to poison, sleep, paralysis, stunning, polymorph, and critical hits.

Reality Sink

Large Outsider
Hit Dice: 9d8+45 (88 hp)
Initiative: +6
Speed: 10 ft. (2 squares), swim 30 ft.
AC: 11 (–1 size, +2 Dex), touch 11, flat-footed 9
Base Attack/Grapple: +9/+13
Attack: Slam +9 touch melee (1d8 negation)
Full Attack: Slam +9 touch melee (1d8 negation)
Space/Reach: 10 ft./5 ft.
Special Attacks: Negation, engulf
Special Qualities: Reality sense 60 ft., immunities, negation, undetectable, ooze-like traits, spell resistance 15
Saves: Fort +13, Ref +8, Will +8

Abilities: Str 10, Dex 15, Con 20, Int 3, Wis 11, Cha 6
Skills: Escape Artist +14, Move Silently +14, Search +9, Swim +12*
Feats: Great Fortitude, Improved Initiative, Iron Will, Toughness
Environment: Aruun waterways
Organization: Solitary
Challenge Rating: 7
Treasure: None
Alignment: Always chaotic neutral
Advancement: 10–18 HD (Large); 19–27 (Huge)
Level Adjustment: —

The surface of the water ahead seems to part in an unnatural manner, as though displaced by an unseen force.

Reality sinks are unnatural, amorphous creatures that can eradicate solid objects with a touch. They are virtually undetectable and thus pose a serious threat to those who encounter them, particularly to those who venture up the rivers that run deep into the Aruun jungle.

No one is quite certain of the origins of these creatures. Some think they are nearly mindless tears in the fabric of reality formed through the excessive use of ancient magics, while others claim they are the result of failed attempts to pierce the veil that separates the mortal world from the celestial realms.

Reality sinks have an affinity for water and other liquids, often immersing themselves in whole or in part. Some speculate the creatures are drawn to fluids as these substances are not subject to the creature's negation ability. Still others believe the creatures are simply looking for hiding places. In any event, reality sinks are skillful swimmers and move quite easily through water and other fluids.

Combat

Reality sinks seem drawn to living creatures, lashing out at them until their targets are completely annihilated by their negation powers or travel beyond the range of their senses, at which point they are promptly forgotten.

Negation (Su): Any solid object or part thereof that comes into contact with a reality sink simply ceases to exist. Wounds caused by the reality sink's slam attack represent entire missing body parts, and as such cannot be healed naturally. Only regeneration or magical healing can heal negation damage.

While reality sinks can be hacked apart with brute force, non-living items that come into contact with them, including weapons, take 1d8 points of negation damage per hit, ignoring hardness. Magic weapons and items receive a DC 19 Fortitude saving throw against this effect. The save DC is Constitution-based.

Engulf (Ex): A reality sink can mow down Medium or smaller creatures as a standard action. It cannot make a slam attack during a round in which it engulfs. The reality sink merely has to move over the opponents, affecting as many as it can cover. Opponents can make opportunity attacks against the reality sink, but if they do so they are not entitled to a saving throw. Those who do not attempt opportunity attacks must succeed at a DC 16 Reflex save or be engulfed; on a successful save, they are able to step or swim back or aside (opponent's choice) as the reality sink moves forward. Engulfed creatures and their possessions are subject to the reality sink's negation ability each round, and are considered to be grappled and trapped within its body. The save DC is Dexterity-based.

Reality Sense (Su): A reality sink has an innate ability to detect moving solid objects (generally living creatures) within 60 feet. It has no other physical senses and is effectively blind if this ability is negated, such as by an *antimagic field*, or if its prey moves beyond this range.

Immunities (Ex): As they don't rely on any other senses, reality sinks are immune to gaze attacks, visual effects, illusions, and other attack forms that rely on sight. Further, the alien mind of a reality sink is immune to all mind-affecting effects (charms, compulsions, phantasms, patterns, and morale effects). Reality sinks are also immune to nonmagical acids and gases.

Undetectable (Su): Reality sinks are naturally invisible, silenced, and odorless. They may be detected as normal by making Spot checks (DC 20 to notice their presence within 30 ft., DC 40 to pinpoint their location). Whenever a reality sink uses its negation ability or takes damage, it becomes visible for a brief instant. If the reality sink is subject to a spell or other effect that deals continuous damage, then it is visible for the duration of the spell or effect. Readied attacks against the reality sink, taken at those moments when it is visible, suffer no miss chance.

The presence of a reality sink may also be detected by observing the environment around the creature, especially when it is in water. A fully submerged reality sink is entirely visible with a DC 20 Spot check, gaining no miss chance, whereas a partially submerged reality sink appears as a visible recess on the water's surface with a DC 15 Spot check, retaining only a 20% miss chance.

Ooze-like Traits: A reality sink is immune to poison, *sleep*, paralysis, stunning and polymorphing. Since it has no clear front or back, and no discernable organs, it is not subject to flanking or critical hits.

Tuk

Tiny Outsider
Hit Dice: 1d8–1
Initiative: +3
Speed: 30 ft. (12 squares), climb 20 ft.
AC: 15 (+2 size, +3 Dex), touch 15, flat-footed 12
Base Attack/Grapple: +0/–8
Attack: Claw +6 melee (1d4–3) or spit dart +5 ranged (1d4)
Full Attack: 2 claws +6 melee (1d4–3) or spit dart +5 ranged (1d4)
Space/Reach: 2 ½ ft./0 ft.
Special Attacks: Spit dart, playmate
Special Qualities: Cooperation
Saves: Fort +1, Ref +5, Will +2
Abilities: Str 5, Dex 17, Con 8, Int 9, Wis 11, Cha 8
Skills: Bluff +3, Climb +11, Hide +15, Jump +11, Listen +4, Move Silently +7, Spot +4.
Feats: Weapon Finesse (claw)
Environment: Any
Organization: Pack (6–10)
Challenge Rating: ¼
Treasure: Standard
Alignment: Always evil
Advancement: None

A flurry of stinging darts slice through the air

around you, accompanied by a keening shriek. In the undergrowth around you, wriggling knots of pink flesh dart from cover to cover, bulbous eyes glittering in the gloom.

Tuks were bred by Izrador to act as agents of terror amongst the Danisil. While not terribly fearsome one-on-one, they travel in packs and have an ingrained lust for destroying children. This hatred toward small humanoids was meant to strike at the heart and hope of the free races. Coincidentally, it gives tuks a fervant hatred of other small humanoids, as well, like halflings and gnomes. To them, small is small.

Combat

Tuks know they are no match for larger enemies alone, so they have developed extremely efficient tactics for fighting as a team. They attack at range, hiding behind cover as they attack with a hail of spit darts.

Spit Dart (Ex): Tuks' teeth grow at an incredible rate, enabling them to grind off tiny shards of enamel, which are then expectorated at targets with great force. These darts have a range increment of 20 ft., and there is no limit to the number of spit darts a given tuk can eject in a day. Spit darts do not receive the normal Strength penalty for thrown weapons.

Cooperation (Ex): Tuks rely on one another for survival and, as a result, have perfected their group fighting tactics. Any tuk can use the aid another action to assist another tuk within 30 ft. Though normally only possible in melee, tuks may use this action against opponents at range and to assist tuks that are at range, as long as all opponents and allies involved are within 30 ft. There is no limit to the number of tuks that can coordinate their attacks in this way, making them surprisingly effective foes when gathered together.

Playmate (Ex): Though tuks look like wriggling knots of flesh with tooth-ringed proboscis to adults, children see them in a considerably different light. To children, tuks seem like small, friendly creatures. This allows tuks to lure children to them and even to manipulate them for extended periods before killing them. Clever and mischievous tuks have convinced children that their parents were actually possessed by demons, and a few have even gotten particularly gullible children to murder their siblings or other loved ones. When a nest of tuks come to roost in a town, one of the first signs is often strange behavior from the children, who become sullen and angry to their parents and others close to them. More than one village of Danisil has been completely destroyed when tuks turned the children against their parents, convincing them to sabotage the town's defenses, set homes alight, poison food and water supplies, and lead adults into the lairs of dangerous predators. Elven legends speak of the Angry Ones, children driven mad by the tuks' deceptions, who lurk within the Aruun and weave elaborate plots of vengeance against tuks and elves alike.

Chapter Two

Creatures of Eredane

Bitterwind

Medium Elemental (Cold, Air)
Hit Dice: 8d8+16 (52 hp)
Initiative: +8
Speed: Fly 60 ft. (12 squares)
AC: 18 (+4 Dex, +4 deflection), touch 14, flat-footed 14
Base Attack/Grapple: +6/+6
Attack: Slam +9 melee (1d8 cold, 1 point Constitution damage)
Full Attack: Slam +9 melee (1d8 cold, 1 point Constitution damage)
Space/Reach: 5 ft./5 ft.
Special Attacks: Constitution damage, debris burst
Special Qualities: Damage reduction 5/mithril, blindsense, cold subtype, elemental qualities, natural invisibility
Saves: Fort +4, Ref +10, Will +4
Abilities: Str 10, Dex 19, Con 14, Int 6, Wis 14, Cha 12
Skills: Listen +9, Move Silently +5, Spot +9
Feats: Alertness, Improved Initiative, Weapon Finesse (slam)
Environment: Any arctic, cold, or temperate
Organization: Solitary
Challenge Rating: 6
Treasure: Standard
Alignment: Usually neutral evil
Advancement: 9–16 HD (Large), 17–24 HD (Huge)

The air around you becomes chill. A dry hiss echoes off nearby stones. Suddenly the wind takes on direction and purpose, becoming a marrow-freezing lance of pain, rifling though your body for some unspeakable purpose.

Orcs and Dorns both tell stories of these strange, seemingly demonic spirits. Dorns claim they are manifestations of local deities, sent to weed out the weak and foolish who fail to learn the harsh lessons of the North. Orcs claim something similar, seeing the bitterwinds as a creation of Izrador sent to test an adult orc's hunting prowess. Surviving an encounter with one of these creatures is seen as a mark of strength in either culture.

In truth, bitterwinds are the murderous, decaying remains of air elementals that have been trapped on Aryth since the Sundering. Unlike their younger brethren, these spirits can just barely maintain a physical form. The most observant adventurer may notice a faint swirl of wind before they strike, or hear the dry hissing of their voices as they mutter to themselves about all of the things lost to time and divine arrogance.

Although they once exclusively inhabited the North, bitterwinds traveled south behind the wave of devastation brought on by the Shadow's armies. They haunt the lonely places between the last fading lights of civilization, striking down the incautious. Like their cousins the earthbacks, bitterwinds rely on the life force and arcane energy of other living beings to sustain their existence. Unlike the earthbacks, however, bitterwinds drain that energy in the form of warmth. Unwary orcs, humans, and fey alike fall prey to the creatures' hunger.

Some legates, having learned of the bitterwinds' taste for life, leave crippled or maimed prisoners for bitterwinds to feed on. Although the spirits cannot be directly commanded, they can be trained to recognize that staying in certain areas will guarantee them plentiful sustenance. This tactic allows legates to lure the creatures into use as wardens to prevent access to conquered buildings, sites, or mountain passes that they can't spare soldiers to guard. Though unreliable, this method is sometimes used to cover the supply lines of Izrador's armies so that the legate in command may take his full army forward, seeking greater glory and prestige.

For reasons unknown, bitterwinds seem to have a fear of running water, sometimes refusing to cross it even when prey is at hand.

Combat

Bitterwinds rely on their invisibility and incorporeal nature to launch devastating attacks against their foes. They typically wait until their target engages in some strenuous or precarious activity (fighting, climbing, running) before attacking. When fighting, the creatures hiss and mutter to themselves in their dry, airy voices.

Blindsense (Ex): Bitterwinds see partly in the infrared spectrum, detecting living creatures by their warmth. Masking one's body temperature with frozen clothing, hiding under snow, and diving into frigid water are traditional ways of escaping a bitterwind's notice, though such desperate actions can just as easily lead to death by exposure.

Natural Invisibility (Su): As beings made completely of air, bitterwinds are nearly invisible, even while attacking. Air temperature drops noticeably within 30 ft. of the creature, however, which may alert savvy adventurers to its presence. The debris and swirling wind accompanying its movement also makes the bitterwind's exact location easier to pinpoint with a Spot check (DC 20) than is usual for invisible creatures. Characters must make this Spot check every time the bitterwind moves.

Divination spells like *see invisibility* and *true seeing* reveal the creature's location, while cancellation effects like *invisibility purge* do not.

Constitution Drain (Su): Living creatures hit by a bitterwind's slam attack must make a DC 16 Fortitude save or suffer 1 point of Constitution damage. For each point of Constitution damage dealt, the bitterwind heals 5 hit points. The bitterwind may accumulate hit points beyond its maximum, but these are termporary hit points that fade at a rate of one per hour.

Debris Burst (Su): As a standard action, a bitterwind may gather loose materials (dust, ice-crystals, rocks, sand, etc.) within its form. On the next round it may send the materials swirling about the surrounding area in a freezing burst of debris and shrapnel, doing 4d6 points of slashing damage and 2d6 points of cold damage to all creatures in a 60 ft. radius spread. A DC 18 Reflex save halves the damage. The saving throw DC is Dexterity-based.

When the bitterwind sweeps up the materials, it becomes visible until the debris burst on the following round. If it opts not to make the attack, the debris clatters to the ground. The attack leaves a very distinctive wound pattern of scarring and frostbite that any Dorn or orc will immediately recognize.

Blight Ogre

Large Giant
Hit Dice: 12d8+60 (114 hp)
Initiative: +0
Speed: 40 ft. (8 squares)
AC: 19 (–1 size, +10 natural), touch 9, flat-footed 19
Base Attack/Grapple: +9/+21
Attack: Bone spur +17 (1d8+8+2d6 unholy+1d6 acid/19–20/x2)
Full Attack: 2 bone spurs +17 melee (1d8+8+2d6 unholy+1d6 acid/19–20/x2)
Space/Reach: 10 ft./10 ft.
Special Attacks: Challenging bellow
Special Qualities: Devil's blood
Saves: Fort +13, Ref +4, Will +5
Abilities: Str 27, Dex 10, Con 20, Int 11, Wis 12, Cha 11
Skills: Climb +16, Jump +16, Listen +8, Spot +8
Feats: Cleave, Great Cleave, Power Attack, Improved Critical (bone spur), Improved Sunder
Environment: Any
Organization: Solitary, pair, or squad (3–8)
Challenge Rating: 8
Treasure: None
Alignment: Always chaotic evil
Advancement: —

Exuding a terrible stench, the powerful ogre crashes forward on legs covered with suppurating sores. Its massive hands are covered with horny protrusions that drip a steaming black ichor, which leaves behind burnt earth where it falls to the ground. Though clearly once an ogre, this creature is now much more.

Blight ogres are the creation of a powerful conclave of orc shamans. Captive ogres are chained in enormous pits into which the witch doctors pour foul-smelling brews and the blood of dozens of sacrifices. Rituals wrung from captured lore pools are used to complete the process, and hideously transformed ogres emerge from the pit, ready to do Izrador's bidding.

Other blight ogre creations are surely in the works, far to the north where the few forces of good cannot disrupt them. Some in the resistance movement are considering traveling deep into enemy territory to assassinate the shamans that perform the creation rituals. Such a mission, while suicide, would greatly aid the cause of both dwarves and elves in their besieged homelands.

Combat

Given their size and racial tendencies, blight ogres are prone to simply stomping across a battlefield and laying waste to anything that gets in their way. But they are also gifted with powerful ways to demoralize their foes and erode their defenses, making them far more deadly than simple berserk warriors.

Challenging Bellow (Ex): A blight ogre's voice is harsh and enormously loud, allowing it to be heard over the din of battle. When it roars, the effect can be devastating to the morale of those who face the creature in battle, causing them to quiver in bowel-loosening horror at the sound.

Using this ability is a full-round action, during which the blight ogre raises its face to the heavens and unleashes a hellish howl of rage and hunger. Those within a 50 ft. radius of the ogre must immediately make a DC 16 Will save or suffer a –4 morale penalty to all attack and damage rolls, saving throws, and skill checks as their primal fear takes hold. This effect persists as long as the blight ogre remains conscious and within sight of the affected creature. The save DC is Charisma-based.

Devil's Blood (Ex): As a result of their transformation, great calcified spurs have burst from the hands and arms of the blight ogres, and their blood coats these natural weapons like a black sheen. The bone spurs are considered *unholy acid burst* weapons.

Blight ogres' acid is also so powerful that it inflicts normal acid damage, rather than half, against stone, wood, or metal objects or structures, including armor and weapons. Blight ogres are therefore regularly employed to destroy defenses and pitted against well-armed and armored squads of dwarves.

Any melee attack against a blight ogre that results in a critical hit showers the attacker with the ogre's blood, causing 2d6 points of acid damage.

Carrion Stag

Large Magical Beast
Hit Dice: 6d10+18 (51 hp)
Initiative: +3
Speed: 50 ft. (10 squares)
AC: 17 (–1 size, +2 Dex, +6 natural), touch 11, flat-footed 15
Base Attacks/Grapple: +6/+10
Attack: Gore +10 melee (1d8+4)
Full Attack: Gore +10 melee (1d8+4), 2 hooves +5 melee (1d4+2)
Space/Reach: 10 ft./5 ft.
Special Attacks: Charging gore
Special Qualities: Scent
Saves: Fort +8, Ref +8, Will +5
Abilities: Str 18, Dex 16, Con 17, Int 4, Wis 16, Cha 4
Skills: Hide –1*, Listen +6, Move Silently +6, Spot +6, Survival +3*
Feats: Dodge, Mobility, Spring Attack
Environment: Forest or plains
Organization: Solitary, pair, or herd (1 male, 4–6 females)
Challenge Rating: 3
Treasure: None
Alignment: Always neutral
Advancement: 7–12 HD (Large)

The thick scent of rotted meat precedes the great stag charging towards you. Rotted filth chokes its reddish fur, while identifiable bits of gristle and gore dangle from a noble rack of antlers.

Carrion stags are a disturbing example of the effects of Fell on a normal ecosystem. These creatures, perhaps through magic, perhaps simply through generations of habit, have become adept predators of the Fell. The rotting meat is apparently an excellent source of protein for the nomadic herds during the winter months, and the fact that it is mobile is even more convenient for these bizarre creatures.

Because even females have horns, the traditional reference to male ungulates, stag, has been applied to entire species. Male carrion stags are over five feet high at the shoulder and weight upwards of 800 lbs. Females are typically slightly shorter, coming to just under five feet at the shoulder and weighting no more than 700 lbs. They have reddish fur with a white underbelly. This fur becomes thicker in the winter months or in cold climates, growing as long as eight inches. During the summer their coat is no longer than one inch. Close examination reveals that a carrion stag bears slightly serrated teeth.

Carrion stags typically travel in small herds, roaming the countryside looking for their preferred meals of moldering flesh. The stags seek out the rankest bodies available. Reliable witnesses claim that they even roll about on the bodies before eating them, perhaps as a way to mark their territory.

Unlike normal animals, carrion stags have no fear of the Fell. In fact, they find the corporeal undead a convenient and mobile form of sustenance. A risen corpse tends to protect itself from smaller scavengers, eventually reaching an advanced state of decay that carrion stags find particularly tasty and easy to digest. The Fell also eventually become abominably stupid; although not overly intelligent themselves, the carrion stags have developed a number of simple hunting methods to trick their even more dimwitted prey.

Alpha males are always at least 9 Hit Dice and have the Track feat.

Combat

Carrion stags prefer to herd Fell with them as they migrate throughout the forests and mountains of the North, but attack humans when Fell are scarce. When facing multiple opponents, the alpha male of the herd selects a single target for elimination. The other deer attack that target with their Spring Attack feat, darting in and out of combat range in an attempt to draw the defenders apart. Once an opponent is sufficiently wounded, the stags charge en masse, hoping to overwhelm the target.

Carrion stags do not eat their humanoid kills immediately. Instead, they wait to see if the creature will rise as a Fell. If it does, then they shepherd it to the nearest collection of Fell, creating a reserve for their future use. If it does not rise, they eat the corpse after it reaches a sufficient state of decay. This usually takes 2d4 days, although colder and dryer environments extend that time.

Charging Gore (Ex): When charging, a carrion stag deals double damage with its gore attack.

Skills: A carrion stag has a +14 racial bonus on Hide checks when in forests. Alpha males have a +12 racial bonus to Survival when tracking Fell by scent.

Degenerate Darghuul

Huge Aberration
Hit Dice: 17d8+170 (246 hp)
Initiative: –3
Speed: 20 ft. (4 squares)
AC: 13 (–4 size, –3 Dex, +10 natural armor), touch 3, flat-footed 13
Base Attack/Grapple: +12/+31
Attack: Greatclub appendage +23 melee (4d6+16)
Full Attack: Greatclub appendage +23/+18/+13 (4d6+16)
Space/Reach: 15 ft./15 ft.
Special Attacks: Engulfing will, gaze of unfathomable depths, roar of the abyss, froth of delirium
Special Qualities: Darkvision 60 ft., dreams of lost aeons, siren's burbling
Saves: Fort +15, Ref –2, Will +10
Abilities: Str 32, Dex 5, Con 30, Int 14, Wis 11, Cha 24
Skills: Bluff +27, Diplomacy +27, Sense Motive +20, Spot +20
Feats: Cleave, Combat Expertise, Great Cleave, Improved Sunder, Improved Trip, Power Attack
Environment: Any
Organization: Solitary
Challenge Rating: 20
Treasure: None
Alignment: Always chaotic evil
Advancement: —

A rough, oily mound of flesh looms above you, its surface swarming with spidery blue and yellow veins. Curds of greenish fat ooze from the corners of eyes the size of shields, while dozens of pupils dilate and contract as if focusing on objects both near and incredibly distant. Arms and legs like tree trunks splay out from the grotesque bulk of the body, frantically rubbing together with wet, squelching sounds.

Before the elder fey wandered the earth, it was the playground for strange and horrible beings. Hidden in the depths of ancient temples and forgotten catacombs, the darghuul were an alien but highly developed race that ruled over vast subterranean kingdoms in those times. Little is known about them; they left behind only impenetrable hieroglyphics and runes, architecture that defies logic, and the degenerate darghuul.

Dwarves believe that the degenerate darghuul are not a true member of that prehistoric race, but rather a species of servitors or abominations imprisoned by them. Whatever the case, the degenerate darghuul are horrors that even Izrador has chosen to avoid, for their wrath is terrible to behold and their madness infectious. While only of average or better intelligence, their minds are unfathomable to fey, human, and dark lord alike, and their purposes are known only to them.

Combat

While they appear to be too slow and bloated to move, degenerate darghuul are quite capable of running and even sprinting. They tend to use their spell-like and supernatural abilities first, then wade into melee with something that looks like a gargantuan two-handed greatclub of flesh and bone extending from two of their upper limbs. The greatclub appendage acts like a weapon except that it may not be disarmed or sundered.

Dreams of Lost Aeons (Sp): Darghuuls' minds travel the dreams of mortals, floating through the consciousness of every race on Aryth. Once per year when one of them finds a mind that intrigues it, a degenerate darghuul may cast a *dream* spell on a target in an attempt to lure it into its lair deep under the earth. Promises of great power, immense treasure, and even weapons capable of defeating Izrador are common in these dreams, and more than one group of heroes have followed them to their fatal end.

Engulfing Will (Sp): Degenerate darghuuls have immense power to control others, and may cast *dominate monster* (DC 22) four times per day. The degenerate darghuul is treated as if it speaks a language understood by the creature, for purposes of this ability only. Caster level 17, save DC is Charisma-based.

Froth of Delirium (Ex): When angered, hurt, or excited, a degenerate darghuul exudes a sticky froth from the surface of its body. The gooey substance splatters outward to fill a five-foot radius surrounding the darghuul and splashes over anyone who performs a melee attack against the creature. The froth contains a powerful intoxicating poison that is absorbed on contact. Those who enter the froth or are splashed by it must make a successful Fortitude save each time they are exposed. The poison is DC 28, initial and secondary damage 1d6 Int. The save DC is Constitution-based.

Gaze of Unfathomable Depths (Su): The darghuuls have existed for tens of thousands of years and have seen things other creatures cannot imagine. Once per day as a full-round action, a degenerate darghuul can open wide the pupils of its massive eyes and show others a hideous glimpse of its own memories. All creatures in a 30 ft. cone must make a DC 25 Will save or suffer

2d6 points of Wisdom drain. Those who are reduced to zero Wisdom effectively acquire the zombie template (see Creating a Zombie, MM) and are under the control of the degenerate darghuul until such time as their Wisdom is raised above 0. If a creature's Wisdom is raised above 0, it returns to normal. The save DC is Charisma-based.

Roar of the Abyss (Su): When angered, the degenerate darghuul can emit a thunderous roar that evokes feelings of primal terror in those who hear it. All creatures within 100 feet of the darghuul when it unleashes this roar must make a DC 25 Will save or cower for 1d6 rounds, after which they are entitled to another DC 25 Will save. Those who succeed at the second save may act normally, while those who fail this save fall into a catatonic state from which they do not emerge for 2d12 hours. The saved DC is Charisma-based.

Siren's Burbling (Sp): Oncer per week, a degenerate darghuul is able to emanate feelings of euphoria and desire to a single living creature that comes within five miles of its lair. No save is immediately required, and the creature may follow or ignore the feelings as it wishes. The feelings grow more intense the closer one gets to the darghuul's resting place, reaching a peak when the darghuul comes within sight, at which point a saving throw is required. This is otherwise identical to a *sympathy* spell (DC 25). Those who fail their saving throw upon seeing the darghuul attempt to move closer to the alien beast, venturing into its lair and snuggling up to the repulsive creature as quickly as possible. The save DC is Charisma-based.

Earthback

Medium Elemental (earth)
Hit Dice: 8d8+40 (76 hp)
Initiative: +1
Speed: 20 ft. (4 squares), burrow 30 ft.
AC: 24 (+1 Dex, +13 natural), touch 11, flat-footed 18
Base Attack/Grapple: +6/+14
Attack: Slam +10 melee (1d8+4)
Full Attack: 2 Slams +10 melee (1d8+4)
Space/Reach: 5 ft./5 ft.
Special Attacks: Improved grab, blood drain
Special Qualities: Scent channeler, elemental fury, elemental qualities
Saves: Fort +13, Ref +3, Will +2
Abilities: Str 18, Dex 13, Con 20, Int 14, Wis 13, Cha 8
Skills: Bluff +12, Hide +1*, Listen +9, Spot +9, Knowledge (history) +10, Knowledge (local) +10
Feats: Great Fortitude, Improved Grapple, Skill Focus (Bluff)
Environment: Hills, Plains, or Mountains
Organization: Solitary
Challenge Rating: 5
Treasure: Standard
Alignment: Usually neutral evil
Advancement: 8–12 HD (medium), 13–24 HD (large)

The earth before you boils up, rocks and soil stained with thickened blood as they form into a man-like creature lunging towards you. It utters, hollowly and sadly, "I need to kill you, now."

These humanoid earthen creatures appear far more demonic than elemental. Standing seven feet tall at full height, they typically hunch so as to appear less than six feet in height. Their front half looks fairly human, with stony skin and the withered features of an ancient man. This humanlike exterior fades away at the edges into the creature's back of earth and stone. Short weathered spikes of stone stand out from the creature's spine. The rock and soil of its back is soaked a viscous black with old blood.

Earthbacks, though commonly referred to as some type of demon or spirit of the earth, are in actuality elementals. Trapped in Aryth after the Sundering, many elemental beings went into deep slumber to conserve their power. Some wandered the world for a time, then embedded their beings, inanimate but still aware, into natural features of significant arcane power. A handful fell under the seeping corruption of the Shadow. These elementals turned to vampirism and predation, sucking power from the souls of their kills. In time they began to kill for enjoyment as well as for sustenance.

Earth elementals that took this path became earthbacks. They drain blood from their targets, storing it within their bodies to savor while waiting for fresh prey. Curiously, some earthbacks developed a taste for conversation as well as blood. The centuries of draining mortals' essential energy slowly imprinted something of mortal concerns upon them. These earthbacks take an interest in history and culture, although they filter this interest though inhuman perception. Particularly active and powerful earthbacks retain a vast repository of historical information. Many are the tales of these terrifying creatures looming up out of the ground before a young Dornish maiden, who then uses her wit and knowledge of her people's culture to appease the demon.

Combat

Earthbacks possess an acute awareness of their own fragility and mortality, and as such do not engage in direct combat if they can avoid it. Instead, earthbacks favor ambush. They wander behind the armies of the Shadow, relying on chaos to cover their activities. An earthback frequently sets up ambush points near shrouded wells, isolated streams, and other places to which intelligent creatures typically come alone. When a vulnerable creature comes close enough, the earthback emerges from the earth. If it is fairly confident that the prey cannot escape, and the victim seems sufficiently terrorized, the earthback may play with its victim for some time. It might let the creature run in several directions, rising from the ground before it each time just when it thinks it has escaped; or perhaps it tells its victim that it will let him live if he can entertain the earthback with local gossip and tales, but then kills the tale-teller anyway.

Scent Channeler (Su): Earthbacks find the blood of channelers to be particularly tasty. As a free action, an earthback may determine if anyone within 30 ft. has the Magecraft feat.

Elemental Fury (Su): When an earthback takes half its normal hit points worth of damage in a single encounter, it enters an elemental rage. Thick, rotted blood erupts from its pores and from around edges of the stones on its back, and the creature trembles with unholy fury. For the rest of the combat, the earthback gains a bonus to attack and damage rolls equal to half its Hit Dice.

Improved Grab (Ex): To use this ability, the earthback must hit with both slam attacks. It can then attempt to start a grapple as a free action without provoking an attack of opportunity.

Blood Drain (Ex): An earthback can absorb blood from its living victims' pores by pinning an opponent. As soon as an opponent is pinned, and every round thereafter, the earthback deals 1 point of Constitution drain. For point of Constitution drained, the earthback gains 5 temporary hit points.

Skills and Feats: Earthbacks can become as still as the stone they come from. An earthback may settle down into the earth as a full-round action, gaining a +15 circumstance bonus on Hide checks. Once the earthback becomes still, any movement breaks the effect. Earthbacks are also considered to have the Improved Unarmed Strike feat for purposes of qualifying for the Improved Grapple feat.

Forsaken

In a life beset with turmoil and horror, humans and fey look to their children as one of their few hopes. While some question the wisdom of bringing a new life into a world under the Shadow's rule, most of the remaining free people see the coming of a child as a good omen, a sign that the free spirit cannot be overcome or denied.

Now however, tales have begun to reach the Court of the Witch Queen of chilling increases in the number of stillborn infants across Eredane. More terrible yet is the corresponding increase in rumors of the demonic possession of newborns and of dark vigils stood at the sides of birthing beds by armed men ready to kill such infants.

The dark truth would shatter even the strongest spirit. As the Shadow rose, so too did the necromantic forces that fueled the Fell. As the years pass, more and more of the dead rise as horrors that live only to feast on the living. In the last days of Aryth, even a mother's womb cannot protect her child from the Shadow.

There is a small chance that any fetus that dies during the pregnancy will awaken into a hideous state of half-life. Called the forsaken, these creatures continue on in a parody of natural growth and birth. The creature feeds for months off of the blood of its mother. It seems to grow normally despite its undead state. Some mothers may feel something wrong during the first few months, then descend into progressively worse states of pain and wretchedness as the birth nears. The last week of these doomed pregnancies becomes a nightmare of sickness and pain. The mother slips into a fever, then a coma, as the rotting creature within her spreads its filth into her veins. More ill-fated are those mothers-to-be who experience only some faintness and assume it is a normal effect of the pregnancy; these are unwarned of the horror that will soon emerge from their bodies. In either case, when the forsaken finishes feeding off its host, it claws its way out in search of additional food.

Upon first glance, the newly born forsaken resembles any other infant member of its species. Within an hour, however, it grows to the size of a small child, its undead organs and rotted muscles bursting from the living sack of skin that disguised it. Once revealed, it consumes whatever meat it can find.

"Adult" forsaken appear to be pre-pubescent children of their race, their bodies in a constant flux of undead and living features, including fresh-flowing blood, rotted flesh, and working organs. When damaged, the creature regenerates new, healthy flesh that may live for several hours or may necrose in seconds. Unlike many undead creatures, the forsaken feels both the wounds it suffers and the constant re-growth and death of its flesh.

Some forsaken develop twisted features, useless limbs, or other physical deformities as their regeneration spirals out of control. These oddities typically develop after a prolonged period of feeding, but always rot off in a few days.

In combat, the forsaken relies on its regenerative power and talon-like claws to rend its foes. Its most horrible weapon, however, is its ravenous maw. The creature attacks with little stealth and almost no tactics. It exists simply to feed in the most effective way possible.

The forsaken continue until finally put to rest. For all practical purposes they seem to be immortal, although it may be that the living parts of their body die from old age.

Creating a Forsaken

Forsaken is an inherited template that can be applied to any newborn humanoid creature (referred to hereafter as the base creature). They appear most commonly among peoples with high birth rates: orcs, humans, gnomes, and halflings. Elves and dwarves may give birth to forsaken; such situations are very uncommon, but these people's rare births make the tragedy that much more horrific. A forsaken has all the base creature's statistics and special abilities except as noted here.

Size and Type: The creature's type changes to undead. Size is always Small.

Hit Dice: Add +12 Hit Dice; increase all current and future Hit Dice to d12s.

Speed: 15 ft. (3 squares); forsaken never grow out of that "awkward" stage.

Armor Class: The creature's natural armor increases by +9.

Attack: A forsaken grows small claws and a monstrous maw, the latter of which is the more fearsome weapon. The bite attack is the primary attack, and does 2d6 points of damage plus Strength modifier. The two claw attacks are secondary attacks, and deal 1d4 points of damage plus one-half Strength modifier. Forsaken use the undead base attack bonus progression (same as wizard).

Special Attacks: A forsaken retains all the base creature's special attacks and gains those described below. Save DCs are equal to 10 +1/2 the forsaken's HD + the forsaken's Cha modifier unless otherwise noted.

Necrotic Poison (Ex): The claws of a forsaken carry a toxic mix of blood and rot into their victims. This causes the victim's flesh to regenerate and necrose just like the forsaken's, except that the effect is much more damaging to a living body. If the victim fails a Fortitude save, he suffers 1d4 Con damage and gains regeneration 1 (silver, acid, and fire deal normal damage) for one hour. Each hour thereafter until the poison is removed from his system or a successful Fortitude save is made, the victim suffers an additional 1d4 points of Con damage and the regeneration effect continues.

Attach (Ex): If the forsaken hits with its bite attack, it may latch onto one of its opponent's limbs (limb determined randomly) and begin devouring it. An attached forsaken is effectively grappling its prey. The forsaken loses its Dexterity bonus to AC, but holds on with great tenacity. Forsaken have a +12 racial bonus on grapple checks.

An attached forsaken can be struck with a light weapon or grappled itself. To remove an attached forsaken through grappling, the opponent must achieve a pin against it.

Devour (Ex): An attached forsaken gnaws at its prey, dealing bite damage in any round that it begins its turn attached to a victim. If the forsaken does damage with its devouring ability equal to ¼ of the victim's maximum hit points, it has severed the limb. The victim suffers one point of Constitution damage each round until the wound is bound with a Heal check (DC 20) or a healing spell.

Horrific Visage (Su): Any living creature within 30 ft. of the forsaken must make a Will save. On a failure, creatures that have one half the forsaken's Hit Dice or less are panicked for 1d4 rounds, suffer 1d4 points of Intelligence damage, 1d4 points of Wisdom damage, and 1d4 points of Charisma damage, and must flee if able. Creatures that have more than half the forsaken's

Hit Dice are immune to the panic effect, but still suffer the ability damage on a failed save. The save DC is equal to 10 + 1/2 the forsaken's HD + the forsaken's Cha modifier.

Special Qualities: A forsaken retains all the base creature's special qualities and gains scent, undead qualities, and those qualities described below.

Detect Life (Su): As a full round action, a forsaken can detect living creatures within 60 ft. The forsaken gains a general idea of the creatures' directions, as well as how many are in the area, but cannot pinpoint the creatures' locations.

Light Sensitive (Su): The forsaken is sensitive to light. It suffers a –1 penalty to all attack rolls when exposed to bright light (anything over torchlight) and a –2 penalty to attack rolls when exposed to full sunlight.

Regeneration 5 (Su): Silver weapons, fire, and acid deal normal damage to a forsaken. If a forsaken loses a limb or body part, the lost portion regrows in 3d6 minutes. The creature can reattach the severed member instantly by holding it to the stump.

Abilities: Str +12, Dex +8, Con —, Int –4, Wis –2, Cha +4

Skills: Forsaken have a +8 racial bonus to Climb, Hide, Jump, Listen, Move Silently, and Spot checks. Otherwise same as base creature. Forsaken should be assigned skill points as normal for undead for all additional Hit Dice. Their class skills are Bluff, Climb, Hide, Jump, Listen, Move Silently, Search, Spot, Swim, Survival.

Feats: Blind-Fight, Iron Will, Multiattack, Toughness, Track

Environment: Any
Organization: Solitary
Challenge Rating: Same as base creature +9
Alignment: Always neutral evil
Advancement: 13–22 HD (Small)

Ogre Damen

Large Giant
Hit Dice: 5d8+15 (37 hp)
Initiative: +1
Speed: 30 ft. (6 squares)
AC: 15 (–1 size, +1 Dex, +5 natural), touch 10, flat-footed 15
Base Attack/Grapple: +3/+13
Attack: Large dagger +9 melee (1d6+6) or large sling +4 ranged (1d6+6)
Full Attack: Large dagger +9 melee (1d6+6) or large sling +4 ranged (1d6+6)
Space/Reach: 10 ft./10 ft.
Special Attacks: Beguiling gaze, spell-like abilities
Special Qualities: Beguile giants, damen's glamour, spell resistance 19
Saves: Fort +7, Ref +2, Will +4
Abilities: Str 22, Dex 13, Con 17, Int 14, Wis 16, Cha 21

Skills: Bluff +11, Craft (sculpture) +6, Diplomacy +11, Knowledge (arcana) +8, Knowledge (history) +8, Knowledge (nature) +8

Feats: Skill Focus (Diplomacy), Ability Focus (beguile giants)

Environment: Cold or temperate hills or mountains
Organization: Solitary (80% chance of 2–10 ogres or trolls) or damen/daughter pair (5th-level charismatic channeler ogre damen, 1 ogre damen, and 4–20 ogres or trolls)
Challenge Rating: 5
Treasure: Standard
Alignment: Usually lawful evil
Advancement: By character class
Level Adjustment: +3

The stooped ogre woman lifts up her face, peering at you though the cascade of her tangled auburn hair. Shockingly beautiful purple eyes lock with yours as her lush lips begin to whisper words of . . .

At first glance, the ogre damen appears to be a normal female of the brutish giant race. Standing anywhere between 9 and 10 ft. tall and weighing up to 300 lbs., ogre damens blend in with other ogres. However, more careful inspection reveals that ogre damens are a breed apart: their grotesquely statuesque figures are strangely beautiful, their lush, tangled red hair bespeaks wildness and passion, and their purple eyes are captivating.

Ogre damens represent a legacy from the ancient past, a bloodline and a secret handed down though generations of corrupted giant society. They work diligently to expand their influence among their own kind, trading companionship and favors for promises of loyalty. The damens do not lead war-bands or fight on the front lines; rather, they work behind the scenes to increase their personal power.

Although cruel and cunning by nature, ogre damens possess long-range planning skills rarely displayed by others of their kind. They also turn their cunning to subterfuge rather than ambush; the damens rarely carry out plans if success is not almost certain.

Combat

Ogre damens rarely engage in direct combat. If attacked, they command their ogre or troll consorts to protect them. If forced to fight, they use their magic and spell-like abilities first, then resort to ranged attacks. If the fight turns against them, damens do everything in their power to escape. In the grand scheme of the giant race, they believe the loss of a few consorts to be a fair exchange for their own survival.

Consorts accompanying an ogre damen have access to several carved wooden and stone minor charms to augment their combat abilities.

Any of the ogre damen's abilities that affect crea-

Ogre Damen Society

In the glory days of the First Age, after the Sundering and before the rise of Izrador, a coven of giant-folk witches gathered in the Highorn Mountains. In their desire for power, they invoked ancient mysteries best left untouched. They bargained with their lives and their souls, exchanging their entire race for personal immortality and dominion.

They spent unchanging centuries seducing and corrupting the giant folk, committing them one by one to the Shadow's twisted schemes. After the last of the great giant folk fell, the dark god betrayed the witches. He transformed them into mockeries of their former beauty, forced to serve as concubines and whores for the people they betrayed.

The witches retained some small measure of their power. In order to survive, they submitted to the curse placed upon them. Each witch also swore, however, to bear a single daughter to whom she would pass her knowledge and power. By the end of the Second Age, rumors circulated though the world of a hidden people among the ogres, matriarchs of their race who could bend the giants to their will.

In this last age the ogre damens still bide their time. They gather small groups of followers, always careful to hide themselves from the Order of Shadow. Although an isolated ogre damen is occasionally found and killed in a chance encounter with a legate or demon, they have for the most part been successful.

Each ogre damen may have countless children; only one female child bears the thick red hair that marks her as a worthy successor, however. That child, called the daughter, serves as the damen's apprentice until the ogre damen grows weary with this world. At that point the damen passes her collection of knowledge and magical charms to the daughter, a rite that ends with the daughter ritually sacrificing her mother to the powers of darkness.

Ogre Damens as Characters

Ogre damens favor the channeler class. They rarely take up the path of the barbarian or wildlander. Ogre damen channelers work hard to conceal themselves from the legates, fearing that Izrador will snatch from them what limited power they have gathered.

tures with the giant type also affect characters with the giant-blooded heroic path, even if their creature type is not giant.

Beguiling Gaze (Su): Any intelligent creature within 30 ft. is subject to the ogre damen's beguiling gaze (see Gaze, Glossary, MM). Targets must make a DC 19 Will save. Non-giants that fail are dazed for 1d4 rounds. Creatures with the giant type that fail are affected as if by a *charm monster* spell with a duration of one day per point of the ogre damen's Charisma modifier. At the end of the duration, the target's attitude toward the ogre damen returns to normal, though the target does not remember that he was ensorcelled. This is a mind-affecting ability. Caster level 7. The save DC is Charisma-based.

Damen's Glamour (Su): This effect surrounds the ogre damen with a permanent *sanctuary* spell (DC 17), but only against creatures of the giant type and only for those giants against whom she has not taken any offensive action. Caster level 7. The save DC is Charisma-based.

Spell-like abilities (Sp): At will—*daze* (DC 15), *levitate, mage hand, obscuring mist;* 3/day—*charm animal* (DC 16), *charm person* (DC 16), *daze monster* (DC 17), *faerie fire, hold person* (DC 18); 1/day—*charm monster* (DC 19), *suggestion* (DC 18). Caster level 7. The save DCs are Charisma-based.

Otherworlders

There are as many types of strange and enigmatic creatures trapped on Aryth by the Sundering as there are trees in the Whispering Wood. While many have fallen to the ravages of war, time, and despair, still there are many outsiders who walk among the folk of Eredane.

Before the Sundering, these creatures were both benign and malevolent, working with and against the mortals of the world according to the designs of their masters, who dwelt upon many and distant planes. Now, adrift and without the guidance of those overlords, their goals range from the esoteric to the world-altering. Some are quiet, unassuming, and hidden, never revealing their nature. Others relentlessly pursue mysterious goals, and show up time and again in the oral histories of the cultures they visit.

Otherworlders' corporeal forms are as varied as their mindsets. They generally take the form of normal people or animals, though some have chosen monstrous or alien shapes. There are tales of otherworlders taking different forms over the ages, while others seem to take the same form each time they appear, but never age.

Apply one of the following templates to any living creature to form an otherworlder. Note that in each of the templates, there are additional entries for "Duty" and "Trigger." These entries describe the purpose of the otherworlder and the ways in which it attempts to fulfill this purpose. Information on resisting the Duty is also found in this section, though few can stand against the desire of the Otherworlders for long. Triggers are events or circumstances which can activate a Duty—whenever an otherworld encounters one of its triggers, it must either attempt to resist the Duty or fulfill it immediately.

Otherworlders often take class levels to improve their abilities (berskers become barbarians, menders become channelers, etc.).

The Berserk

Filled with a lust for blood and the rush of battle, the berserk is an otherworlder most often found at sites where great physical violence might occur, though it need not be a great battle. A berserk might hire its services out to resistance fighters, letting itself be slaughtered over and over again in hopeless battles against Izrador; it might let itself be captured for use in a gladiatorial arena; or it might become a hunter-killer for the legates.

Creating a Berserk

"Berserk" is a template that can be added to any living creature with a Strength of at least 13 (referred to hereafter as the base creature). A berserk uses all the base creature's statistics and special abilities except as noted here.

Size and Type: The creature's type changes to outsider. Size is unchanged, as are most features (base attack bonus, saves, skill points per Hit Die, etc.).

Hit Dice: Increase to d12.

Speed: Same as the base creature.

Armor Class: The base creature's natural armor improves by +4.

Special Qualities: The berserk has all the special qualities of the base creature, plus the following special qualities.

Unstoppable (Ex): The berserk does not feel pain and does not die as easily as others. The berserk may continue fighting or acting normally until reduced to –10 hit points, at which point it dies outright.

Strength of the Berserk (Ex): When a berserk suffers more than 10 hit points of damage from a single attack, it becomes extremely aggressive and will attack the damage dealer with great ferocity. This state of berserk anger remains in effect for 1d4 rounds, after which the berserk loses its benefits.

While under the effects of the strength of the berserk, the creature gains the following:

- +4 Strength
- The Improved Critical Feat with the weapon currently being wielded
- Damage Reduction 5/—

Abilities: Change from the base creature as follows: Str +4, Dex +4, Con +4, Int –2, Wis –2, Cha –2.

Feats: The berserk gains the Cleave, Power Attack, and Whirlwind Attack feats, even if it does not fulfill the prerequisites for them.

Climate: Any.

Organization: Always solitary.

Challenge Rating: As base creature +2.

Treasure: One-half standard.

Alignment: Chaotic neutral, neutral, or lawful neutral.

Duty

The berserk was once a proud warrior whose entire existence was fighting for its master's cause. With no cause now to truly believe in, berserks retain their sanity by focusing on fighting as much, and as hard, as they can. This means that they have a strong tendency to battle on the side of the underdog. Berserks often seek out resistance groups, throwing themselves into the fray against Izrador's minions. On the other hand, more than one orc tribe has been rescued from complete obliteration by elven raiders when a berserk appeared in orc form and rallied the tribe to victory. The berserk spirit wishes to expand conflict and promotes violence as the ultimate answer to all conflict. The berserk's duty, then, often leads it to fight against the local power and to lead others to fight against authority as well.

Resisting this Duty is very difficult. Berserks must make a DC 20 Will save to avoid reacting to the triggers below. When his duty is triggered, the berserk must resort to some violent action to defeat the creature or force that incited the trigger. This can take the form of simply killing the creature, but could also mean an attack against the creature's possessions, or the incitement of those in the area to rise up and strike down the offender.

Triggers

- The striking of a helpless creature.
- An attack against the person of the berserk.
- A strong military presence (in this case, the berserk may take a longer term approach to fulfilling its duty, but must be constantly striving to bring about conflict, with the goal of disrupting the military presence).

The Herald

These otherworlders were messengers of the higher planes, delivering the voice of the divine from on high. They often oppose berserks, as they were created to prevent conflict by opening lines of communication. In days past, the fey begged these creatures to carry missives from one location to another, and there are still those who remember that offering a herald a small token can guarantee the delivery of a message to the intended recipient.

But the legates have learned of this secret, as well, and fervently seek out heralds to use for their own dark purposes. Perhaps most vile of all, the legates have sent several good-aligned heralds to their death by invoking their duties and tasking them to deliver messages to encampments thick with orcs.

Creating a Herald

"Herald" is a template that can be added to any creature (referred to hereafter as the base creature). A herald uses all the base creature's statistics and special abilities except as noted here.

Size and Type: The creature's type changes to outsider. Size is unchanged, as are most features (base attack bonus, saves, skill points per Hit Die, etc.).

Speed: Same as the base creature +10 feet. If the base creature has any special movement modes, the herald retains these abilities. In addition, the base creature receives a +10 racial bonus on Climb and Swim checks. Finally, base creatures without flight as an ability are considered to be permanently under the effect of an *air walk* spell (Caster level = Hit Dice of the herald).

Special Qualities: The herald has all the special qualities of the base creature, plus the following special qualities.

Discern Location (Su): Once per day, the herald may use the *discern location* spell to find its message's recipient, except that it need not have seen the creature it is attempting to find nor possess some item that once belonged to it.

Untrackable (Ex): The herald moves through terrain at all times as if affected by a *pass without trace* spell. The herald never radiates a magical aura.

Tireless (Su): The herald never needs to sleep or eat, and may travel up to 16 hours per day without rest.

Eye of the Owl (Su): The herald gains low-light vision.

Abilities: Change from the base creature as follows: Dex +4, Con +4, Int +4.

Feats: The herald gains the Inconspicuous feat as a bonus feat.

Climate: Any.

Organization: Always solitary.

Challenge Rating: As base creature +1.

Treasure: Standard; gems, jewelry, and tokens only.

Alignment: Any

Duty

The herald is charged with carrying messages from one person to another; once offered a token of personal significance, the herald attempts to carry any written or spoken message to the target. The message can be spoken (up to five minutes in length) or up to three written pages of material. Heralds are not duty-bound to carry packages along with messages, but may choose to do so if they wish.

While under the compulsion of this duty, the herald must make all haste to the message's intended recipient. Resisting this duty is difficult. Heralds must make a DC 15 Will save to avoid reacting to the trigger. When this duty is triggered, the herald must leave within the hour and proceed toward his target as outlined above.

Trigger

- Being offered a token of personal significance. When the herald is offered the item, he must accept and respond by saying, "What is your message?"

The Mender

Menders are those who were once charged by their patron deities with spreading healing and succor across the world in their names. While they may once have had a great plan to bring peace to the entire world, the loss of their connection to their masters has left these otherworlders without any real direction. They move from town to town, attempting to heal the injured and soothe the raging spirits they encounter.

Creating a Mender

"Mender" is a template that can be added to any creature (referred to hereafter as the base creature). A mender uses all the base creature's statistics and special abilities except as noted here.

Size and Type: The creature's type changes to outsider. Size is unchanged, as are most features (base attack bonus, saves, skill points per Hit Die, etc.).

Special Attacks: A mender retains all the special attacks of the base creature, as well as those detailed below. All special attacks have a DC of 10 + ½ the mender's HD + its Charisma modifier.

Pacifying Touch (Su): As a melee touch attack, the mender may sap a creature of the will to fight. This attack causes no damage, but targets who fail their Will save are subjected to a targeted *calm emotions* spell with a duration of 1 round per Hit Die of the mender. The mender need not concentrate to maintain this effect.

Pacifying Speech (Su): Once per week, a mender may attempt to pacify a large group of people. This effect is identical to the *enthrall* spell, except that after 10 minutes of speaking, listening creatures must make another Will save; those that fail are considered fascinated, and may be influenced just as if they were under the effect of a *hypnotism* spell.

Special Qualities: The mender has all the special qualities of the base creature, plus the following special qualities.

Lay on Hands (Su): A mender may heal the injuries of others with a touch, restoring a total number of hit points each day equal to twice its Hit Dice x its Charisma bonus. A mender may choose to divide its healing among multiple recipients, and it doesn't have to use it all at once. Using lay on hands is a standard action.

Purify Body (Su): Three times per day, a mender may purify a patient's body, using either a *neutralize poison, remove disease,* or *restoration* effect as per the spell. Caster level is equal to the mender's Hit Dice.

Harmless Visage (Su): This ability may be used three times per day as a free action. When the mender activates this ability, it becomes completely forgettable and innocuous in appearance. This effect lasts for 10 minutes per Hit Die of the mender. Creatures that fail a Will save (DC = 10 +1/2 the mender's HD + Charisma modifier) can not only not attack the mender, but also forget about its existence. This effect is broken if the mender takes an offensive action within the creature's presence, but otherwise the creature's recollection of any of the mender's actions slowly fades into vague nothings over the next few days.

Abilities: +4 Dexterity, +4 Wisdom, +4 Charisma.

Skills: The mender receives a +10 insight bonus on Heal and Profession (Herbalism) checks; otherwise same as base creature.

Environment: Any.
Organization: Always solitary.
Challenge Rating: As base creature +1.
Treasure: Standard.
Alignment: Usually good.

Duty

The mender is sworn to preserve life and stop conflict whenever possible. Though it can fight to defend itself, attacking with anything other than its pacifying touch is very difficult, requiring a DC 20 Will save. The mender must instead heal those in need or help others avoid conflict, even if they do not wish to themselves. Menders may unfortunately be manipulated by evil; a classic example is the tale of Algothon Blacktongue, who was dispatched by the Night King Jahzir to forge a lasting peace between two warring tribes of orcs, uniting them so they could be more easily brought beneath the banner of Izrador.

Whenever possible, a mender must use its abilities to heal any wounded or ill creatures that it sees. A mender that wishes to avoid healing a creature must make a DC 30 Will save to avoid fulfilling this duty. Even if the save is successful, the mender suffers a –4 penalty to all skill checks, attack rolls, and saving throws for 1d4 days following this denial of its duty.

Triggers

- Seeing or hearing of a sick or dying intelligent creature.
- Seeing or hearing of a conflict that could be resolved peacefully.
- Seeing or hearing of a community in turmoil.

The Warden

Wardens were once sacred guards and defenders. Because the holy sites they were sworn to defend were destroyed in the Sundering or the chaos that ensued, these otherworlders are perhaps the most aimless of their kind. Most have taken on new areas to protect, though their alien minds seem to have latched onto the idea of terrain types rather than specific locations.

Creating a Warden

"Warden" is a template that can be added to any creature (referred to hereafter as the base creature). A herald uses all the base creature's statistics and special abilities except as noted here.

Size and Type: The creature's type changes to outsider. Size is unchanged, as are most features (base attack bonus, saves, skill points per Hit Die, etc.).

Armor Class: Natural armor improves by +4.

Attacks: A warden retains all the attacks of the base creature.

Special Qualities: The warden retains all the special qualities of the base creature and those listed below.

Chosen Environment: The warden must choose one of the terrain types detailed in Geography, Chapter 6, DMG.

Strength of the Land (Su): While within its chosen environment, the warden gains fast healing 5 and he receives a +4 bonus to Strength, Dexterity, and Constitution. In addition, the warden need not eat or drink while within its terrain.

Sense of the Land (Su): While within its chosen environment, the warden may make a DC 15 Spot check whenever an animate creature of any type (including incorporeal creatures) comes within one mile of its current location. If the creature is actively damaging the area, the warden receives a +5 insight bonus on this skill check.

One With the Land (Su): The warden may not be attacked by any natural (that is, non-magical) animals that reside in its chosen environment. The warden is likewise unable to attack the creatures that reside within in its selected environment.

Abilities: See strength of the land, above.

Skills: The warden receives a +10 insight bonus on Balance, Climb, Hide, Jump, Knowledge (local), Knowledge (nature), Listen, Move Silently, Spot, Swim, and Survival checks while within his chosen environment.

Feats: The warden gains the Track feat.

Climate: Any.

Organization: Always solitary.

Challenge Rating: As base creature +1.

Treasure: None.

Alignment: As base creature, usually non-evil.

Duty

The warden is sworn to preserve and protect a specific type of terrain, typically the type of terrain in which its original charge was located. When passing through or near this type of terrain, the warden feels drawn to the plants and animals that live within its bounds. Any warden who passes into his selected environment must spend no less than 24 hours in that environment, looking for damage to it or signs of an incursion of hostile creatures. If the warden finds anyone damaging the environment or its inhabitants, he must attempt to drive them from the bounds of the environment, even at the cost of his own life.

The warden must make a DC 30 Will save if it wishes to avoid fulfilling this duty. Even if the save is successful, the warden suffers a –4 penalty to all skill checks, attack rolls, and saving throws for 1d4 days following this denial of its duty.

Triggers

- The unnecessary killing of a creature within the bounds of his chosen environment.
- Damage to the chosen environment.

The warden does not consider creatures who live in harmony with the environment to be damaging it and attempts to ascertain the intent of creatures before launching into a full-scale assault on them. Finding a village of fisherman, for example, is not the same as uncovering a legion of the Shadow's soldiers attempting to deforest an area for siege engines.

Puppeteer

Medium Aberration
Hit Dice: 11d8+77 (126 hp)
Initiative: –2
Speed: 15 ft. (3 squares)
AC: 11 (–2 Dex, +3 natural), touch 8, flat-footed 11
Base Attack/Grapple: +8/+9
Attack: Bite +9 melee (2d4+1)
Full Attack: Bite +9 melee (2d4+1) and 4 claws +7/+7/+7/+7 melee (1d4)
Space/Reach: 5 ft./5 ft. (15 ft. with claws)
Special Attacks: Absorption, infection, poisonous spray
Special Qualities: Camouflage
Saves: Fort +10, Ref +1, Will +7
Abilities: Str 12, Dex 7, Con 24, Int 19, Wis 11, Cha 17
Skills: Bluff +19, Gather Information +17, Hide –2, Intimidate +19, Listen +14, Search +18, Sense Motive +17
Feats: Combat Expertise, Combat Reflexes, Multiattack, Persuasive
Environment: Any
Organization: Solitary or clutch (10–12)
Challenge Rating: 9
Treasure: None
Alignment: Always evil
Advancement: By class

A mass of swollen, greyish tissue, surmounted by a slobbering mouth, seems to be the center of this creature. Blackened appendages, stick-thin and serrated at the tip, emerge from this central mass in dizzying profusion, folding and unfolding jerkily as it jitters toward you.

Puppeteers are a hideous race of beings created by the ancient Darghuul. After their creators met their mysterious end, the puppeteers brooded for thousands of years, locked in icy fortresses in the far north. Minions of the Shadow set these creatures free and, to show their gratitude, the puppeteers have been faithful servants of Izrador ever since. Though amorphous and distinctly alien in appearance, puppeteers are masters of deception, able to easily change the coloration and texture of their bodies to become virtually invisible.

Even more dangerous, however, is their ability to infect others with a bit of their own tissue, seizing control of the infected target and directing him to act as Izrador wishes. This ability destroyed the dwarven Black Rock Clan entirely, and is rumored to be behind the destruction of other villages and isolated towns throughout Aryth. Only knowledge and careful protections can thwart the plans of these creatures, who are even now spreading across the land to do the bidding of their dark master.

Combat

While slow and not terribly strong, puppeteers have several alien and fearsome special abilities. They attempt to stay as far from combat as possible, instead directing their puppets to defend and attack.

Absorption (Ex): The puppeteers are able to quickly recycle the flesh of other creatures to repair damage to their own bodies. Whenever the puppeteer causes damage to a living creature with a bite attack, it heals itself by the same amount. Thus, a bite that deals 6 points of damage to a target heals the puppeteer by 6 hit points, as well. A puppeteer may never exceed its maximum normal hit points using this ability.

Camouflage (Ex): The puppeteer is able to change its natural coloration and alter its skin texture, giving it a +20 racial bonus on Hide checks when underground or in dim lighting.

Infection (Su): To attempt to infect a target, the puppeteer must first successfully hit the target with a claw. If the target takes damage from the claw attack, it must make a DC 21 Fortitude save with a circumstance penalty equal to the damage caused. If the save succeeds, the infection is thwarted, though the puppeteer may attempt to infect the target again. If the save fails, the target is infected, and falls under the sway of the puppeteer in a number of rounds equal to 1d4 + the target's Constitution modifier.

Infected creatures become an extension of the puppeteer's consciousness; it can direct their actions as a free action, and they may use the puppeteer's skill ranks instead of their own. As per the *domination* spell, however, subjects forced to take actions against their natures receive new saving throws with a +2 bonus. A puppeteer may never gain control over more creatures at once than it has Hit Dice. As the infection is organic, it cannot be blocked with *protection from evil* or similar spells. The save DC is Constitution-based.

It is important to note that this ability works on all organic creatures, living or dead, including undead with corporeal bodies. A zombie can be infected just as easily as a halfling. Additionally, this ability works on non-humanoids, and is not restricted by size, Hit Dice, or levels.

A creature that moves more than five miles from the puppeteer that infected it, and remains more than five miles away for a full 24 hours, is freed from infection, as the puppeteer tissue loses contact with its master and withers away. The only other ways an infected creature may be freed are by killing the puppeteer that infected it or by receiving a *remove disease* spell from a caster of a level equal to or higher than the puppeteer's Hit Dice.

Fortunately, it is possible to protect oneself from infection by ingesting a tea containing ground silver. Any who ingest the tea are immune to a puppeteer's infection for 24 hours afterwards. A single teaspoon of silver (roughly 3 sp) can produce enough tea to protect four Medium or smaller creatures or two Large creatures.

To discover this tidbit of information requires a DC 30 Knowledge (history) or Knowledge (arcana) check, and preparing it accurately requires a DC 30 Knowledge (nature) or Profession (herbalist) check.

Poisonous Spray (Ex): A puppeteer can eject a 30 ft. cone of poisonous mucous once every 2d4 rounds. The poison is contact, Fortitude DC 21, initial damage 1d6 temporary Dex, secondary damage 2d6 temporary Dex. The save DC is Constitution-based.

Razor

Medium Outsider
Hit Dice: 14d8+56 (119 hp)
Initiative: +8
Speed: 50 ft. (10 squares), Climb 50 ft.
AC: 22 (+4 Dex, +8 natural), touch 14, flat-footed 18
Base Attack/Grapple: +14/+21
Attack: Claw +22 melee (2d6+7/19–20/x2) or flame +18 ranged touch (1d6+5)
Full Attack: 2 claws +22 melee (2d6+7/19–20/x2) or flame +18/+13/+8 ranged touch (1d6+5)
Space/Reach: 5 ft./5 ft.
Special Attacks: —
Special Qualities: Blood charm, body riding, dam-

age reduction 10/magic, razor seed, scent, spell-like abilities, spider climb, immune to fire

Saves: Fort +13, Ref +13, Will +9

Abilities: Str 25, Dex 18, Con 18, Int 14, Wis 11, Cha 15

Skills: Knowledge (arcana) +9, Knowledge (history) +9, Hide +21, Jump +24, Listen +17, Move Silently +21, Spellcraft +17, Spot +17, Survival + 17, Swim +24, Tumble +21

Feats: Combat Expertise, Improved Critical (claw), Improved Initiative, Track, Weapon Focus (claw)

Environment: Any

Organization: Solitary, pair, squad (4–6 plus 2 1st–3rd level orc barbarians per razor), or unit (8–30 plus 2 1st–3rd level orc barbarians per razor)

Challenge Rating: 13

Treasure: None

Alignment: Always neutral evil

Advancement: 15–28 HD (Medium)

You catch sight of faint glimmers in the darkness. Just as your eyes resolve them into a manlike shape, the creature falls upon you. Long, rending talons reach out towards your beating heart while unearthly cries fill the air, edged with a hunger that can only feed on hot blood.

Razors are man-like demons, usually standing no more than 7 ft. tall. They have mostly human features, although their skin is dark gray and their eyes are shards of midnight glass with glowing silver pupils. These demons derive their name from the long obsidian talons that rip though their fingertips. Similar shards of obsidian are laced through their gray skin, emerging no more than one inch from the skin's surface.

Unlike most of Izrador's servants, the razors served the dark god long before his fall to Aryth. They were part of his infernal host when he challenged the gods. These demonic essences fell with him, and they realized that their bodies of darkness and evil could not continue to exist indefinitely in this new organic world. Rather than die, they enacted a bold and vile plan. Using the last of their remaining corporeal days, the razors captured and interbred with as many fey females as they could find. They then performed a horrid ritual that only one out of every four of them survived. When all was said and done, the razors had gained the ability to possess any creature that bore even a trace of their blood, enabling them to continue on in this lesser world.

Combat

Razors are Izrador's personal shock troops, sent by the god himself to deal with special problems. Centuries of training, combat, and dedication have honed their fighting skills and tactics to an unholy edge. Although they enjoy blood and torment as much as the next demon, their fierce loyalty to the Shadow prevents them from diverting from their mission. If engaged in combat outside of their mission parameters, razors are efficient and calm, dealing with their foes as quickly as possible so they can continue to their target. When that target is finally within their grasp, however, their demonic heritage emerges: They gore, torture, and mutilate their targets, bathing themselves in blood and pain, before finally delivering the killing blow.

Even a single razor represents a deadly threat to even experienced parties of resistance fighters. Unfortunately for the resistance, razors usually travel in numbers. Whether encountered alone, in a pair, as part of a squad, or as an element in a larger unit, razors work together in the most effective way possible. These demons have known each other for centuries; they know the way each member of the unit thinks and fights, allowing them to respond to and support one another as if they had a single mind.

A pair of razors is usually a hunting or assassination team sent after a specific target, usually an important part of the resistance command structure. Pairs avoid contact with bystanders whenever possible, preferring to locate the target and dispatch it with a minimal amount of resistance. A squad of razors (usually 4 to 6 of the creatures) may also be assigned to deal with a particularly difficult skirmish situation. Entire units of razors are reserved for breaking specific areas or winning key battles. In all cases, the creatures move at great speed to reach their objective, then set to work with vigor. When breaking resistance in an area, they destroy everything and everyone they encounter. When sent to turn the tide of a battle, they ignore the orders of the local commanders, waiting for the moment when an application of elite force will do the most good.

Any group of razors larger than two will have at least twice their number of orc barbarian warriors with them. These orcs stay out of the fighting if they can, although they attack downed or badly wounded opponents. They are highly mobile, extremely tough, and take a continuously defensive stance; they must stay alive, waiting for the moment when one of their masters fall. As soon as this occurs, the nearest orc steps forward, taking the razor seed into his body and allowing the infernal creature to be born anew.

Blood Charm (Su): As a standard action, a razor may cast *dominate person* on a creature that carries razor blood (see below). The target must make a DC 19 Will save to resist the effect. Caster level 14, save DC is Charisma-based.

Razor Seed (Su): When razors die, their host bodies dissolve into a pile of rotted, festering meat. Within the pile is a six-inch diameter, glossy black orb called a razor seed. The razor seed has hardness 10 and 40 hit points. Although fully aware, the razor seed cannot use any of its spell-like abilities other than *body riding*. Razors can only create seeds when they fully control a host body; if the host body dies during the transformation process, then the razor dies a true death as well.

If a creature touches a razor seed, the razor may attempt to transfer its essence and, if it succeeds, may transform its host immediately instead of waiting for a full day (see below).

Body Riding (Su): As a full round action, a razor who has been "killed" may transfer its essence into any creature bearing razor blood within 10 ft. The creature must make a DC 19 Fortitude save to resist the effect. The save DC is Charisma-based. Once the essence has been transferred, the razor may take over the creature, transforming the new body into a semblance of its old, with normal razor attributes and full hit points. The razor may enact the transformation no sooner than one day after transferring its essence; it may also, however, bide its time, emerging days, weeks, or even years later. Until that time, the host creature has no idea that anything is amiss. Attempts to detect evil on the host creature will only reveal evil if the host has fewer Hit Dice than the razor; the stronger the host's own sense of self, the more easily the razor can hide within.

When the transformation begins, the target creature writhes in visceral torment as its body changes to accommodate the demonic possession. The creature's body becomes a fully functional razor as described above within 1d4 rounds. The creature can take no actions during the transformation, and retains all of its attributes until the transformation is complete.

Spell-like Abilities: As a free action, at will—*detect magic, detect good, produce flame*. As a standard action: 3/day—*burning hands* (DC 13), *cure critical wounds, fire shield* (DC 15), *locate creature, scorching ray* (DC 14), and *see invisibility;* 1/day—*true seeing*. Caster level 14, save DCs are Charisma-based.

Spider Climb (Su): Razors have the ability to rapidly scale any surface. They act as though under the effects of a permanent *spider climb* spell (Caster level 14), except that their climb movement is not limited to 20 ft.

Razor Blood

Through their horrid acts after the Sundering, the razors managed to spread their blood to all of the fey races through unwilling interbreeding. Over the years, the taint of their blood spread thoughout the lands. Any fey has a .01% chance of having razor blood, plus .01% per Constitution modifier. The character only needs to roll once to determine whether or not his blood carries the razors' curse.

Sundered Beasts

Outsiders and elementals were not the only ones directly affected by the Sundering. Many magical beasts, previously allies of good, were utterly and forever changed by the alteration of magic on Aryth.

Gloom Hound

Medium Magical Beast
Hit Dice: 6d10+6 (39 hp)
Initiative: +7
Speed: 40 ft. (8 squares)
AC: 17 (+3 Dex, +4 natural), touch 13, flat-footed 14
Base Attacks/Grapple: +9
Attack: Bite +7 melee (1d6+1)
Full Attack: Bite +7 melee (1d6+1)
Space/Reach: 5 ft./5 ft.
Special Attacks: Howl of despair, improved flanking, rage, spell-like abilities, trip
Special Qualities: Scent
Saves: Fort +6, Ref +8, Will +0
Abilities: Str 13, Dex 17, Con 12, Int 10, Wis 6, Cha 11
Skills: Hide +12, Move Silently +12
Feats: Improved Initiative, Run, Weapon Focus (bite)
Environment: Any temperate land
Organization: Solitary, pair, or pack (7–16)
Challenge Rating: 4
Treasure: None
Alignment: Usually chaotic evil
Advancement: 7–12 HD (Medium); 13–18 HD (Large)

The slavering dog has mangy fur, a gaunt form, and bloodied teeth. Its eyes roll madly in its head as it lopes toward you, and a low moaning howl begins to seep from its mouth.

When the Sundering trapped outsiders on Aryth and blocked extradimensional travel, it also altered reality for the once-benign race of blink dogs. These magical canine creatures, once playful and good, found themselves permanently trapped on this plane, unable to use the blink ability that came as naturally to them as flying does to an eagle. It wasn't long before the creatures went mad with despair and longing.

Gloom hounds have ashen-brown fur and are larger and stockier than other kinds of wild dogs. They travel in packs lead by the strongest of their kind. Fights and power struggles among pack members are common, and usually end with fresh meat to be shared by the remainder of the pack. Gloom hounds have a strong taste for freshly killed meat and a preference for fey in particular. Though cunning at times, their behavior generally borders on paranoia and madness.

Gloom hounds speak their own language, a remnant of that used by their ancestors.

Combat

Gloom hounds are ferocious pack hunters that lay claim to vast territories. Once the pack has chosen its prey, it relentlessly stalks its victims until they grow tired or succumb to the pack's supernatural abilities.

Howl of Despair (Su): Filled with all the despair and hate of its loss, a gloom hound's primal howl can drive those who hear it into a deep despair. Gloom hounds emit the howl constantly, as a free action, whenever they hunt or attack prey. Any creature within 60 ft. of a howling gloom hound must make a DC 13 Will save or be overcome with a deep despair. Those inflicted are shaken for the length of the combat. The save DC is Charisma-based.

Improved Flanking (Ex): As a remnant of the tactics employed by their ancestors, gloom hounds are able to take particular advantage of flanked opponents. Gloom hounds gain a +4 flanking bonus on their attack rolls when flanking an opponent instead of the usual +2.

Rage (Ex): Always teetering on the edge of madness, a gloom hound that takes damage in combat flies into a berserk rage on its turn, clawing and biting madly until either it or its opponent is dead. An enraged gloom hound gains a +4 bonus to Strength, a +4 bonus to Constitution, a +2 bonus to Will saves, and a –2 to AC. The creature cannot end its rage voluntarily.

Spell-like Abilities (Sp): At will—*daze* (DC 10); 1/day—*confusion* (DC 14), *hold monster* (DC 15). Caster level 6. Save DC is Charisma-based.

Trip (Ex): A gloom hound that hits with a bite attack can attempt to trip the opponent (+1 check modifier) as a free action without making a touch attack or provoking an attack of opportunity. If the attempt fails, the opponent cannot react to trip the wolf.

Chapter Two: Creatures of Eredane

Splinter Steed

Large Magical Beast
Hit Dice: 6d10+30 (63 hp)
Initiative: +7
Speed: 60 ft. (12 squares)
AC: 20 (–1 size, +3 Dex, +8 natural), touch 13, flat-footed 17
Base Attack/Grapple: +6/+16
Attack: Magical horn +14 (1d10+7 and horn splinter)
Full Attack: Magical horn +14 (1d10+7 and horn splinter), 2 hooves +7 melee (1d6+3)
Space/Reach: 10 ft./5 ft.
Special Attacks: Horn splinter, spell-like abilities
Special Qualities: Immunities
Saves: Fort +10, Ref +9, Will –1
Abilities: Str 22, Dex 17, Con 21, Int 10, Wis 4, Cha 14
Skills: Bluff +10, Hide +12, Move Silently +12
Feats: Improved Initiative, Power Attack, Weapon Focus (horn)
Environment: Any temperate land
Organization: Solitary, pair, or curse (3–6)
Challenge Rating: 4
Treasure: None
Alignment: Always chaotic neutral
Advancement: 7–12 HD (Large)

The equine beast has a pale coat accented with streaks of gray and black. Atop its forehead is a single, misshapen horn bearing several deep fissures and jagged edges. Upon noticing you it takes an offensive stance, dropping its head to display its horn and haunting black eyes.

Splinter steeds are the sad descendants of the once noble race of unicorns that protected Aryth's deep forests. All of their nobility, goodness, and protective power was destroyed in an instant; when the Sundering occurred, it shattered the horn of every living unicorn on Aryth. The remnants of the race still bear these scars.

The Sundering did much more than deprive the unicorns of their divine gifts and teleportation abilities. Massive conflagrations caused by the ensuing demonic and draconic conflicts claimed the forests these creatures had so long fought to protect. Those forests that survived grew more savage, and the fey that had been the unicorns' closest allies grew more aloof and unreachable. Madness spread like a disease among the race, and despair made them particularly attuned to the foul taint of the Shadow as it spread southward. Over time, the unicorns were transformed. Their isolationist tendencies became paranoia, and the beasts that once spread healing now spread terror.

Splinter steeds are covered in haggard white coats that are pocked with black or silvered streaks. Some are almost entirely ashen or black. Likewise, few of these beasts bear the golden eyes of their ancestors, but instead have eyes of deep obsidian or an oily brown. Their tattered manes are long and wild. The horn of a splinter steed appears misshapen and pocked by flaws. As the splinter steed grows, these flaws become more pronounced, and parts of the beast's horn begin to grow brittle, splinter, and break off. The horn usually grows between two and three feet long. The typical splinter steed adult grows to about eight and one-half feet in length and stands about six feet high at the shoulder.

Combat

Splinter steeds are unpredictable and may attack even if unprovoked. They begin combat by charging if possible, dealing double damage on charges with their horns as if they were lances. The misshapen, fractured horn acts as a +1 magic weapon, though its power fades if removed from the creature.

Horn Splinter (Su): The twisted horn of the splinter steed is constantly fracturing, breaking off, and regrowing. On a successful critical hit against a living foe, 1d10 fragments of the horn become embedded in the opponent, with many possible results. First, the target is suddenly awash in unsettling visions and maddening thoughts, and must make a DC 15 Will save or suffer 1d3 points of Wisdom drain from the onset of madness. The creature continues to suffer 1 point of Wisdom drain on a failed save each day that the fragments remain. In addition, while the fragments remain embedded, the creature is unable to gain restful sleep and wakes fatigued each morning. A DC 18 Heal check, taking one hour, is required to remove each of the fragments.

Spell-like Abilities: At will—*chill touch* (DC 13); 3/day—*ghoul touch* (DC 14), *shatter* (DC 14); 1/day—*contagion* (DC 15), *crushing despair* (DC 16). Caster level 6, save DCs are Charisma-based.

Immunities (Ex): Splinter steeds are immune to all poisons, *sleep*, charm, and hold effects and spells.

Chapter Three

Spirits and Allies

Craft Current

Large Outsider (Incorporeal)
Hit Dice: 10d8+20 (65 hp)
Initiative: +4
Speed: Fly 50 ft. (10 squares)(perfect)
AC: 13 (–1 size, +4 Dex), touch 13, flat-footed 9
Base Attack/Grapple: —
Attack: —
Full Attack: —
Space/Reach: 10 ft./—
Special Attacks: Heat of the forge, spell-like abilities
Special Qualities: Incorporeal, manifest
Saves: Fort +9, Ref +11, Will +5
Abilities: Str —, Dex 18, Con 14, Int 18, Wis 2, Cha 2
Skills: Appraise +17, Craft (any two) +20, Craft (any four) +12, Disable Device +17, Knowledge (architecture and engineering) +20, Open Lock +17, Search +16, Use Rope +17
Feats: Iron Will, Skill Focus (two Craft skills), Skill Focus (Knowledge [architecture and engineering])
Environment: Any
Organization: Solitary
Challenge Rating: 6
Treasure: None
Alignment: Always neutral
Advancement: 11–20 HD (Large)

The tools lying on the ground come to life, chiseling and shaping the blank stone block before you. As you move closer, the work ceases, and a hollow voice emerges from the air to murmur threateningly, "work in progress, do not approach."

For generations, these intelligent, incorporeal workers plied their many trades on Aryth, working tirelessly for the priests that summoned them. More intelligent and capable than the vassal spirits, craft currents were the workmen behind the greatest of temples and the most intricate of carvings.

The Sundering stranded them, but they kept on with their work. Unable to breed on Aryth, they have declined in numbers, but a few can still be found, toiling for those who know the words to say and the sacrifices to offer.

Combat

Craft currents do not like to fight, greatly preferring to create rather than destroy. Still, if pressed into battle, their many spell-like abilities can be used to batter or baffle opponents.

Heat of the Forge (Su): Craft currents can generate intense heat, equal to that found in a blacksmith's furnace or a miner's smelter. This heat is normally focused and released in concentrated bursts for crafting purposes, but may also be used at will to generate an intense blast of heat in a 15-ft. cone. All creatures caught in the cone must make a DC 17 Reflex save or suffer 5d6 points of damage. Those who succeed at their saves suffer only one-half damage from this attack. The save DC is Constitution-based.

Manifest (Su): A craft current can manifest itself as a shapeless force effect, similar to an unseen servant, in order to manipulate tools and perform detail work. It has an effective strength score of 16 for this purpose.

Spell-like Abilities: At will—*acid splash, animate objects, animate rope, chill metal* (DC 16), *consecrate, control water, create water, fabricate, grease* (DC 15), *hallow, heat metal* (DC 16), *knock, make whole, mending, move earth, otiluke's freezing sphere* (DC 20), *ray of frost, rusting grasp, shatter* (DC 16), *shrink item, soften earth and stone, stone shape, telekinesis* (DC 21), *tenser's floating disk, transmute metal to wood, unseen servant, wall of iron* (DC 20), *wall of stone* (DC 19), *warp wood* (DC 16), *wood shape* (DC 16). Caster level 10, save DCs are Intelligence-based.

Guardian Grove (Virenaheen)

The guardian grove, or *virenaheen* in High Elven, is a generic name for any area of the elven homeland that has been enchanted against invaders. Orcs, tellingly, refer to such areas as *ginrifang,* place of the hopeless death. It is said that these plants existed long before the histories of the Third Age. They may even be a remnant of the time before the Sundering. Whatever their history, they are a much-needed boon for the elves.

The size and power of the plants in a guardian wood depend entirely on the amount of magic invested in them. The weaker shrubs and undergrowth may have been enchanted by a wandering channeler to guard his sleep as he passed through the wood, while the most powerful sentinels were probably planted and nurtured by experienced whisper adepts who cultivated them for centuries. Some even have the power to roam, albeit slowly, in ever-shifting lines of offense and defense. All guardian groves are strong contributors to the Whisper. A few examples of guardian grove plants are listed below.

Guardian Grove Traits: The plants in a guardian grove possess the following traits (unless otherwise noted in a creature's entry).
- Plant traits
- Tremorsense
- Damage reduction 3/—

Vigil Vine (Gessidil)

Small Plant
Hit Dice: 1d8+2 (6 hp)
Initiative: 0 ft.
Speed: —
AC: 10 (+1 size, –5 Dex, +4 natural), touch 10, flat-footed 10
Base Attacks/Grapple: –2/–6
Attack: Tendril –2 touch (entangle)
Full Attack: Tendril –2 touch (entangle)
Space/Reach: 5 ft./5 ft.
Special Attack: Entangle
Special Qualities: Camouflage, whisper alarm, guardian grove traits
Saves: Fort +4, Ref +0, Will +0
Abilities: Str 6, Dex —, Con 15, Int —, Wis 11, Cha 9
Environment: Aruun Jungle, Caraheen, Miraleen, Veradeen
Organization: Solitary, bed (3–6), or grove (10–20)

Challenge Rating: 1/4
Treasure: None
Alignment: Neutral
Advancement: 2–4 HD (Small)

You see the orc trod forward, sniffing fearfully, as if it is suspecting your ambush. Before you can spring the trap, however, a vine snakes out from the undergrowth and grabs its ankle. The orc grunts in surprise and begins to struggle as the vine's skin hardens to a thick bark around its leg.

Vigil vines are the first defense against invaders of the forests of the elves. Being mindless, they tend to attack any non-elven humanoid who treads on them.

The shape and coloration of vigil vines vary depending on the season and climate, but all are ground-crawling vines with few leaves and thick, ropey stalks between two and six feet in length.

Combat

These mindless guardians never attack elves, and only attack most other humanoids if they enter the plant's square. The whisper adepts have trained them to go out of their way to attack the forest's ancient enemy, however; orcs are attacked as soon as they move adjacent to the vigil vine.

Entangle (Ex): Vigil vines grow rapidly and drop many seeds, but this fecundity is offset by their high rate of self-destruction. As soon as a vigil vine hits a target, it immediately wraps itself around its victim's leg and dies, its vine stalk hardening to an unmoving and resilient bark. The victim must make a DC 12 Reflex save or be *entangled* as per the spell. The save DC is Constitution-based.

Concealment (Ex): To the untrained, a vigil vine appears to be simply another part of the forest. However, those who make a DC 14 Knowledge (local forest) or Knowledge (nature) check recognize it as a vigil vine when they come within 15 ft.

Whisper Alarm (Su): When a vigil vine catches a non-elven humanoid, it sends out a silent alarm via the Whisper. Anyone within a mile that is able to sense the Whisper may do so with a +2 circumstance bonus on the check. Success means that the character is able to gauge the approximate direction and distance to the vigil vine and its captive, but nothing may be discerned about the captive itself.

Bulwark Hedge (Fillardrya)

Medium Plant
Hit Dice: 4d8+8 (26 hp)
Initiative: +0
Speed: —
AC: 10 (–5 Dex, +5 natural), touch 10, flat-footed 10
Base Attack/Grapple: +3/+3

Attack: tendril +3 touch (bind)
Full Attack: tendril +3 touch (bind)
Space/Reach: 5 ft./5 ft.
Special Attack: Binding
Special Qualities: Blind, camouflage, whisper alarm, guardian grove traits
Saves: Fort +6, Ref +1, Will +1
Abilities: Str 10, Dex —, Con 15, Int —, Wis 11, Cha 9
Environment: Caraheen, Veradeen
Organization: Bed (3–6) or thicket (10–20)
Challenge Rating: 2
Treasure: None
Alignment: Neutral
Advancement: 5–7 HD (Medium); 8–12 (Large); 13–18 (Huge)

You hear the rattling rush of black-barbed arrows bouncing off of the leaves of the bush you crouch in. Its leaves part as you unleash your own storm of iron-tipped shafts into the seething mass of approaching orcs.

A fully-grown bulwark hedge stands seven feet tall. Its glossy green leaves resemble elongated holly leaves. The thin branches of the hedge belie its tenacious strength. Like the holly tree they somewhat resemble, bulwark hedges remain green throughout the year.

These remarkable hedges grow tall and straight along what were once the long fair parkways stretching throughout Erethor. In addition, beds and groves of the bulwark hedges appear at random thoughout the forests. Although they do not appear to grow flowers or fruit, some elven sages theorize that they somehow mysteriously reproduce as the Whisper commands, growing where they are needed.

Combat

Bulwark hedges have two basic functions: concealment and obstruction. Although basically mindless, they can easily recognize the difference between an elf and any other species; non-elves and their weapons are blocked, while elves and their weapons may pass through easily.

Blind (Ex): While a normal hedge might provide concealment, bulwark hedges actively deflect attacks against their elven allies. Any elf may step through a bulwark hedge as part of his normal movement. The hedge grants the elf improved cover against enemies on the other side. This provides a +8 cover bonus to AC, a +10 cover bonus on Hide checks, a +4 cover bonus on Reflex saves against attacks that originate or burst out from a point on the other side of the cover, and effectively gives improved evasion against any attack to which the Reflex save bonus applies. As usual, creatures using the bulwark hedge for cover are not subject to attacks of opportunity; this allows elves to use the hedges as harrowing but effective ambush lanes, step-

ping out in the midst of enemy forces to attack and then moving along the other side of the hedge at a full-out run for their escape. Bulwark hedges never provide cover of any sort to orcs or other evil creatures trying to hide behind them; they also act as an obstacle (see Movement, Chapter 8, PHB) to any such creatures, costing 8 squares (40 ft.) of movement to get through.

Bind (Ex): Bulwark hedges cannot directly inflict damage on their targets. However, on a successful touch attack, they can latch dozens of thin branches around any target of Medium size or smaller within a 5-ft. radius. If the target fails a DC 14 Reflex save, it is pulled into the hedge. A creature trapped in the hedge suffers a –2 penalty to attack rolls, a –4 penalty to effective Dexterity, and cannot move. Each round, the entrapped creature may make a Strength check (DC 20) or an Escape Artist check (DC 25) to escape. A hedge can only contain one creature per 5-foot square. The save DC is Constitution-based.

Camouflage (Ex): To the untrained, a bulwark hedge appears to be simply another part of the forest. However, those who make a DC 16 Knowledge (local forest) or Knowledge (nature) check recognize it as a bulwark hedge when they come within 30 ft.

Whisper Alarm (Su): When a bulwark hedge catches a non-elven humanoid, it sends out a silent alarm via the Whisper. Anyone within two miles that is able to sense the Whisper may do so with a +2 circumstance bonus on the check. Success means that the character is able to gauge the approximate direction and distance to the bulwark hedge and its captive, but nothing may be discerned about the captive itself.

Sentinel Tree (Umannitich)

Huge Plant
Hit Dice: 10d8+110 (155 hp)
Initiative: –5
Speed: 0 ft.
AC: 20 (–2 size, –5 Dex, +17 natural), touch 9, flat-footed 17
Base Attacks/Grapple: +7
Attack: —
Full Attack: —
Space/Reach: 10 ft./15 ft.
Special Attack: Sleep
Special Qualities: Aura, camouflage, whisper alarm, guardian grove traits
Saves: Fort +18, Ref —, Will +8
Abilities: Str —, Dex —, Con 32, Int 14, Wis 21, Cha 16
Environment: Caraheen, Miraleen
Organization: Solitary, row (3–6), or grove (10–20)
Challenge Rating: 7
Treasure: None
Alignment: Neutral
Advancement: 11–20 HD (Gargantuan)

The orcs creep among the towering trees of the forest, growing unease visible in their brutish faces. The leaves above their heads begin to flutter as the wind whispers though them. Gently, the leaves fall, and the heavily armed orcs fall as well.

These ancient trees stand between 20 and 30 feet tall, with large gnarled limbs reaching up to 15 feet from their trunks. Sentinel trees have grooved, silvery bark and wide dark green leaves. Their sap glows faintly with arcane power, giving them a slightly luminescent quality in pitch darkness.

Combat

Sentinel trees do not engage in the vulgar struggle of direct combat. Instead, they quietly rain magical leaves down upon anyone standing under their branches. Any non-elf struck by the leaves falls helpless to the ground. The helpless targets are usually quickly dealt with by forest scavengers or elves looking for a quick and easy kill.

Sleep (Su): The touch of a sentinel tree's leaves brings instant, untroubled slumber to any living creature. Creatures merely walking beneath such a tree have a 20% chance of brushing up against a leaf. Those aware of the tree's abilities may automatically move beneath the tree's 15 ft. radius canopy without brushing against leaves, but the tree may, at its discretion, drop 1d6 leaves on each passerby, each of which makes a +8 touch attack.

Unwilling targets that brush up against or are hit by a leaf must make a DC 20 Will save to resist the effect; elves may automatically succeed, if they wish. Targets that fail fall into a deep slumber lasting for eight hours. Willing targets may choose to fall into slumber without making a Will save; if they accept the sleep, it lasts four hours, after which they awaken fully refreshed. In either case, sleepers should be considered to be under the effect of a *sleep* spell for purposes of being awoken. During their slumber, sleepers see visions of far away lands and events. A skilled scryer (Wisdom check DC 20) can force these visions to show him specific locations or people in the past or present. The save DC is Wisdom-based.

Aura (Su): All sentinel trees radiate an aura that makes evil creatures uneasy and harms evil incorporeal creatures. Every round that an evil creature stands within 30 ft. of a sentinel tree, it must make a DC 15 Will save or become frightened for 2d4 rounds. Every sentinel tree within 30 ft. of the target increases the DC of the Will save by +2. Evil incorporeal creatures, even those inhabiting other creatures' bodies, are subject to the same effects within 60 ft., and also take 1 point of damage per round per sentinel tree within 60 ft.

Camouflage (Ex): To the untrained, a sentinel tree appears to be simply another part of the forest. Those who make a DC 18 Knowledge (local forest) or Knowledge (nature) check recognize it as a sentry tree when they come within 60 feet of it.

Whisper Alarm (Su): When a sentinel tree causes a non-elven humanoid to fall asleep, it sends out a silent alarm via the Whisper. Anyone within three miles that is able to sense the Whisper may do so with a +2 circumstance bonus on the check. Success means that the character is able to gauge the approximate direction and distance to the sentinel tree and its slumbering victims, but nothing may be discerned about the sleeper itself.

Guardian Spirit

Medium Outsider (Incorporeal)
Hit Dice: 8d8 (83 hp)
Initiative: +0
Speed: 30 ft. (6 squares), fly 30 ft. (6 squares) (perfect)
AC: 14 (+1 Dexterity, +3 deflection), touch 16, flat-footed 15
Base Attacks/Grapple: +8/+12
Attack: Force slam +16 melee (2d6)
Full Attack: 2 force slams +16 melee (2d6)
Space/Reach: 5 ft./5 ft.
Special Attacks: —
Special Qualities: Incorporeal, natural invisibility, parry, spell-like abilities
Saves: Fort +6, Ref +14, Will +8
Abilities: Str —, Dex 26, Con 10, Int 5, Wis 10, Cha 16
Skills: Heal +11, Hide +19, Listen +13, Search +8, Spot +13
Feats: Alertness, Combat Reflexes, Iron Will
Environment: Any
Organization: Solitary
Challenge Rating: 8
Treasure: None
Alignment: Always neutral

The air coalesces before you, taking on the shape of a large, heavily armored humanoid. Though it carries no weapon, the size of its shimmering, mail-clad hands seem more than sufficient to cause grievous harm to those who oppose the creature.

Created in ages past, guardian spirits were summoned and trained by powerful wizards to protect important leaders or emissaries. Though the spirit has little ability to think for itself, it reacts with great force to protect the individual it is assigned to protect.

While none of the wizards who created these powerful constructs still live, it is still possible to gain control over one of these creatures. Each was bound to protect the wearer of a small piece of jewelry, most often a ring or brooch. While the jewelry is worn, the guardian spirit does its utmost to protect the wearer.

(essentially, the guardian spirit's attack roll result becomes the charge's Armor Class if it's higher than the charge's regular AC). Because a guardian spirit has the Combat Reflexes feat, it may attempt to parry at any time, even when flat-footed.

Spell-like Abilities: 3/day—*cure minor wounds, illusory wall* (DC 17), *fog cloud, protection from arrows, protection from energy, see invisibility, shield, wind wall.* The *shield* spell may also be cast on the creature the guardian spirit is protecting. Caster level 10, save DC is Charisma-based.

Skills: Because the guardian spirit is incorporeal, it has a limited ability to interact with the material world. It cannot use its Heal skill, for instance, to save its charge directly, but it might be able to use its knowledge to tell a bystander how to bind its charge's wounds or treat him for poisoning.

Heepa—Heepa

Small Fey (Incorporeal)
Hit Dice: 2d6 (7 hp)
Initiative: +2
Speed: Fly 20 ft. (good) (4 squares)
AC: —
Base Attack/Grapple: —
Attack: —
Full Attack: —
Space/Reach: 5 ft./5 ft.
Special Attacks: Spell-like abilities
Special Qualities: Bodiless, spell-like abilities
Saves: Fort +0, Ref +3, Will +3
Abilities: Str 2, Dex 14, Con 10, Int 11, Wis 12, Cha 11
Skills: Listen +6, Spot +6
Feats: Alertness
Environment: Any
Organization: Solitary, band (3–6)
Challenge Rating: ½
Treasure: None
Alignment: Always good
Advancement: —

The child looks up at you with a secret smile. When you ask who she's talking to, she says simply, "my floaty friend."

The heepa-heepa are bodiless fey spirits who watch over the young of creatures great and small. These primitive and noble creatures make no distinction between the type of children they protect, and use their powers to the utmost to defend baby birds, elf toddlers, or abandoned orc infants, all with equal zeal. These ancient spirits were once quite numerous, but the predations of the Shadow in the North have greatly thinned their numbers; brave though they may be, the small fey can do little to protect the world's children during a raging war.

Combat

Guardian spirits are quite powerful, but have very little in the way of tactical knowledge or strategic cunning. Instead, they respond with brute force, using their abilities to dispatch enemies while protecting their charges. It is important to note that guardian spirits do not take orders from those to which they are bonded; they simply do their best to protect the one in their care.

If an individual protected by a guardian spirit is rendered unconscious, the guardian spirit will do its best to defend the fallen individual. If the charge is killed, however, the spirit immediately returns to the item of jewelry from which it was taken. Though it cannot be used for 24 hours, after that time anyone who wears the jewelry will be protected by the guardian spirit for as long as they wear it.

Natural Invisibility (Su): This ability is constant, allowing the guardian spirit to remain invisible even when attacking. This ability cannot be dispelled or circumvented by any spell, including *invisibility purge.*

Parry (Ex): Any physical attack, whether melee or missile, against a guardian spirit's charge provokes an attack of opportunity by the guardian spirit in the form of a parry. The decision to parry must be made before the attack is rolled. The guardian spirit makes an attack roll; if it is greater than the opponent's attack roll, the attack is deflected by the guardian spirit's force slam

Combat

Heepa-heepa attack any who appear intent on harming a child in their presence. They are generally incapable of harming opponents, but they can use their spell-like abilities to distract, frustrate, or scare off would-be attackers. While some members of the band harass the attackers, the others do their best to guide the children to safety.

Bodiless (Su): Heepa-heepas have very little ability to interact with the material world outside of their spell-like abilities. They are always invisible, and are identical to the forces manifested by the *unseen servant* spell for purposes of interacting with material objects and being damaged.

Spell-like Abilities (Sp): Heepa-heepa may cast any 0-level spell (DC 11), as well as *feather fall*, at will. Caster level 1, save DCs are Wisdom-based.

Highland Imp

Small Fey
Hit Dice: 1d6+1 (7 hp)
Initiative: +2
Speed: 30 ft. (6 squares)
AC: 15 (+1 size, +2 Dex, +2 leather), touch 14, flatfooted 13
Base Attack/Grapple: +0/–5
Attack: Dagger –1 melee (1d4–1 and poison) or dart +2 ranged (1d4–1 and poison)
Full Attack: Dagger –1 melee (1d4–1 and poison) or dart +2 ranged (1d4–1 and poison)
Space/Reach: 5 ft./5 ft.
Special Attacks: —
Special Qualities: Charm gift, darkvision 60 ft.
.**Saves:** Fort +1, Ref +5, Will +4
Abilities: Str 8, Dex 14, Con 11, Int 13, Wis 10, Cha 11
Skills: Craft (first) +9, Craft (second) +6, Hide +11, Knowledge (arcana) +7, Knowledge (nature) +7, Move Silently +7, Survival +4
Feats: *Skill Focus (first craft)
Environment: Hills, Plains, Mountains
Organization: Solitary, pair, or band (4–6)
Challenge Rating: 1/2
Treasure: Standard (2x charms)
Alignment: Usually neutral good
Advancement: By character class
Level Adjustment: +0

You catch sight of a small figure that looks much like a thin child as it tries to slip into the shadows. Baggy clothing drapes around the creature's stick-thin limbs as it scurries away.

Highland imps are small fey with large, liquid eyes and pale yellow skin. Their slightly oversized heads totter on the end of thin necks. Most look chronically undernourished, with flaps of flesh hanging from reedlike arms and legs. Imps wear baggy clothing woven from course materials. They also wear carefully tanned leathers under the outer layers of cloth to turn aside attacks.

Most of the fey believe that the highland imps died millennia ago, after Izrador captured the majority of their kind and transformed them into goblins. In truth, a few managed to escape capture, retreating to the deepest warrens of their kind. There they eek out a meager existence, holding on to the last embers of their hope.

The imps were once known as the greatest makers of magical charms and potions in Aryth. They retain only vestiges of their ancient wisdom, using charms to aid them in their day-to-day struggles. Any encounter with them prominently features minor, lesser, and greater charms with a wide variety of powers.

Combat

Highland imps fight only if they have no other choice. If encountered alone, an imp runs for cover as quickly as possible. A pair or group faced with enemies usually splits up, hoping that at least some of their number may escape.

If forced to fight, highland imps strike with daggers and darts covered with a mild paralyzing poison (Injury,

single warren stretches for miles, a complex interweaving of tunnels and small chambers where families dwell. The eldest imp rules the warren, walking the long tunnels every night to ensure that nothing has breached the walls.

All imps learn the ancient secrets of crafting charms. From the cradle to the grave they work with these minor objects, ringing their warrens and dens with charm after charm. These subtle protections keep the Shadow from finding their last refuges.

Highland Imps as Characters

The statistics above are for an imp with one level of expert. Highland imps favor the channeler class, mostly following the hermetic path. Many also take up the wildlander class. Imps typically take the Magecraft and Brew Potion feats regardless of what class they pursue, following the ancient traditions of their people. Imp wildlanders focus on learning how to avoid detection at all costs.

Highland Imp Traits (Ex):
- –2 Str, +2 Dex, +2 Int—Imps are remarkably intelligent, but physically weak
- Darkvision 60 ft.
- Charm Gift
- Automatic Languages—Imp, Goblin. Bonus Languages—Norther, High Elven, Orcish, and Sylvan.
- Favored Class: Channeler.

Leaper (Eagita)

Tiny Magical Beast
Hit Dice: 1/2 d10+1 (3 hp)
Initiative: +3
Speed: 30 ft. (6 squares), glide 60 ft. (12 squares)
AC: 17 (+2 size, +4 Dex, +1 natural), touch 16, flat-footed 13
Base Attack/Grapple: +1/–7
Attack: Claw +1 melee (1d4–2)
Full Attack: 2 claws +1 melee (1d4–2)
Space/Reach: 5 ft./5 ft.
Special Attacks: —
Special Qualities: Glide, leaping, *mage hand*, simple speech
Saves: Fort +2, Ref +6, Will +1
Abilities: Str 6, Dex 18, Con 12, Int 5, Wis 12, Cha 10
Skills: Climb +18, Hide +16, Jump +18, Survival +8
Feats: Dodge
Environment: Caraheen
Organization: Solitary or pair
Challenge Rating: 1/4
Treasure: None
Alignment: Usually neutral good
Advancement: 3–5 HD (tiny)

Fortitude DC 14, initial damage dazed for 2d4 rounds, no secondary damage). Their hollow bone daggers carry enough poison for 4 successful strikes. Their darts can only strike once before needing to be re-coated. Once they daze their enemies, the imps beat a hasty retreat.

If captured, an imp will try to barter whatever charms or potions he has for his life. He will also offer to use his special ability to create a custom charm for his captors. Captured imps never reveal the location of their home warrens, even upon pain of torture and death.

Charm Gift (Su): Highland imps are natural charm crafters (see MN Core Book, page 83). They may take 20 whenever making charms, and only need half the normal number of ranks in Knowledge (arcana) and Knowledge (nature) to make the four levels of charms.

Highland Imp Society

Highland imps are the last remnant of the fey race twisted by Izrador into goblins. Before their fall into Shadow, they were a reclusive race, engaged in little traffic with the outside world. Now they are all but forgotten, hiding in warrens dug deep into the soft soil of their highland homes. They come out only at night, when the pale light of the stars creates deep shadows in which they can hide.

Imp warrens have dozens of hidden entrances, none large enough to admit a Medium or larger creature. A

The squirrel-like creature looks up at you, amusement and nervousness in its eyes. Among the rapid chirps and squeals coming from its open mouth you recognize the words 'here' and 'have.' It holds out a full quiver of arrows, then rushes back to the supply tent.

Leapers look like a cross between a flying squirrel and a kangaroo, with wide membranes stretching between articulated front paws and hind legs. These oversized back legs are somewhat longer than typical for a rodent, giving them an impressive ability to leap long distances at need, and even glide if they jump from elevation. Leapers weigh between 10 and 15 lbs. They can live to be up to 100 years old.

Far back in the First Age, elves bred leapers as pets and companions. Over the ages these helpmates became intensely loyal pets, capable of assisting their masters with a variety of simple chores. Some time during the Second Age, leapers picked up the ability to speak a handful of words from whatever the native language of their master happened to be.

Leapers bond with a single elf for life. This bonding forms the central attachment of their existence. They have no other family or associations. A female leaper occasionally seeks out male companionship, but raises the resulting litter of 2d4 pups by herself. Pups grow up quickly, pair bonding with elven children or adults within six months of birth.

When war came, these gentle, curious creatures proved valuable allies, their unique physiology and skills allowing them to be of great use against the Shadow. Their ability to move quickly and understand simple instructions makes them invaluable to the elven war effort. Leapers typically serve as messengers, carrying notes from one part of the elven army to the other. The bravest of them also carry small supplies (charms and arrows) to embattled fighters on the front lines.

Leapers may be called by elven and elfling channelers as familiars.

Combat

Leapers avoid combat whenever possible. However, if their pair-bonded elf comes under attack, they launch themselves at the attackers with fatal frenzy. Leapers will gladly sacrifice their own lives to allow their elven partner a chance to escape.

Glide (Ex): Leapers can glide at a rate of 40 ft. per round. They lose 5 ft. of altitude per round of gliding.

Leaping (Ex): All Jump checks that leapers make are made as if they had taken a running start.

Mage Hand (Su): Leapers have an innate magical ability to move small objects by force of will. They may use *mage hand* at will.

Simple Speech (Ex): Leapers know up to sixty words of their pair-bonded elf's native language.

Skills: Leapers get a +20 racial bonus on Climb and Jump checks, and a +4 racial bonus on Hide and Survival checks.

Lore Pool

Small Outsider
Hit Dice: 1d8 (4 hp)
Initiative: +0
Speed: 0 ft. (0 squares)
AC: 5, touch 5, flat-footed 5
Base Attack/Grapple: —
Attack: —
Full Attack: —
Space/Reach: 5 ft./0 ft.
Special Attacks: Daunting knowledge
Special Qualities: Vast knowledge, enduring
Saves: Fort +2, Ref —, Will +2
Abilities: Str 1, Dex —, Con 10, Int 18, Wis 10, Cha 2
Skills: Bluff +0, Intimidate +0, Knowledge (any seven) +8, Knowledge (any one) +21, Listen +4, Sense Motive +4
Feats: Skill Focus (primary Knowledge skill)
Environment: Any
Organization: Solitary
Challenge Rating: 1
Treasure: None
Alignment: Always neutral
Advancement: —

A small pool of viscid, purple slime lies within a crystalline basin. A pair of rudimentary eyes emerge from the slightly swirling fluid and blink languidly at you, while a burbling voice emerges from the fluid. "What is it you wish to know?"

Lore pools are a race of outsiders originally sent to Aryth to watch and record the development of the fey races and to absorb what they could of the world's history and culture. The Sundering trapped these small, helpless creatures, who have remained in their hiding places ever since. There is no gravity on their home plane, where they are able to propel themselves from place to place on extruded cilia, but on Aryth they are simply too weak to move.

Lore pools can be found scattered across all of Aryth. Some were found by elves and given new, more comfortable homes in crystalline basins in exchange for providing the elves with their knowledge and other abilities. Still others were captured by the Shadow's minions and coerced into using their abilities for evil. Even more are sequestered across the countryside or in ancient ruins, where they hide and observe the world around them, instinctively collecting knowledge despite being unable to report back to their masters.

Over the years, many isolated lore pools have become antisocial and neurotic. Unable to return home and confined to one spot, they are naturally irritable, grumpy, and prone to irrational temper tantrums. Where they once may have readily provided information, they now must be cajoled or intimidated into revealing what they know to others. They also take a perverse delight in commanding their "mental inferiors" to complete difficult tasks for them, withholding vital information until the job is complete.

Combat

Lore pools are somewhat able to protect themselves from attack using their special abilities. Whenever possible, however, they will attempt to avoid any physical conflict, as they are nearly certain to lose such a contest.

Daunting Knowledge (Sp): As a full-round action, the lore pool may reveal some tidbit (which may not be true) about a target's fate, simulating a *fear* spell (DC 19) against a single target. This ability may not be used more than once per day against a single foe, but may be used at will by the lore pool. Caster level 10, save DC is Intelligence-based.

Vast Knowledge (Sp): Three times per day, the lore pool may cast the *greater scrying* spell (DC 21) and may, if it chooses, display the results of this spell on its surface. Caster level 10, save DC is Intelligence-based.

Enduring (Su): Lore pools do not need to eat, drink, or sleep. There are no limits to their natural lifespan and many trapped on Aryth are thousands of years old.

Skils: Lore pools receive a +10 racial bonus on a single Knowledge skill; this is their area of specialty, and is the same skill to which their Skill Focus feat is applied.

Seedra

Medium Fey (aquatic)
Hit Dice: 5d6 (21 hp)
Initiative: +2
Speed: Swim 60 ft. (12 squares)
AC: 15 (+2 Dex, +3 shell armor), touch 15, flat-footed 12
Base Attack/Grapple: +2/+3
Attack: Shell slash +2 melee (1d6+1) or water javelin +3 ranged (1d6+1)
Full Attack: Shell slash +2 melee (1d6+1) or water javelin +3 ranged (1d6+1)
Space/Reach: 5 ft./5 ft.
Special Attacks: Water javelin
Special Qualities: Aquatic invisibility, blindsight, water shout, wave turmoil
Saves: Fort +1, Ref +8, Will +6
Abilities: Str 12, Dex 14, Con 10, Int 11, Wis 11, Cha 11
Skills: Escape Artist +10, Listen +8, Move Silently +10, Spot +8, Swim +9, Survival +8
Feats: Iron Will, Lightning Reflexes
Environment: Any ocean
Organization: Band (6–8)
Challenge Rating: 2
Treasure: None
Alignment: Always chaotic
Advancement: —

As the waves begin to toss about the skiff, your Mirasil guide looks at you in alarm. "Quick, your cloak, the brightly colored one," she says urgently, "toss it overboard to pacify the seedra!"

The seedra are thought of as spirits of the sea by the sailors and boaters of Aryth. Some say they were once Miransil who took to the sea to explore a relationship with powerful sea spirits. If that is so, their culture did not survive their migration . . . seedra are wild and fey. Although they are invisible when in water, those that have glimpsed the elusive creatures say they are almost shark-like in their sleek, bullet-headed appearance.

Seedra are equally likely to attack or greet those who pass through their territory. Wise sailors have learned to reduce attacks on their boats by painting their hulls bright colors and, more importantly, by throwing trinkets, cloth, meat, and charms over the side of the boat. A half-dozen pounds of common goods is sufficient to grant passage to a large ship or group of travelers, but the seedra have short memories, and it behooves the traveler to move quickly through the region to avoid having to pay the bribe once more.

Combat

Seedra never leave the sea to attack enemies. When in the water, they lash out with the invisible razor-edged shells with which they decorate their unseen bodies.

Water Javelin (Su): Seedra can create one javelin per round from sea water as a free action. A javelin may only be thrown by the seedra who creates it. They have normal range increments in both water and air.

Blindsight (Ex): Seedra use echolocation to sense creatures and objects within 120 ft. underwater.

Water Shout (Ex): Like dolphins or whales, seedra are able to communicate across vast distances thanks to their ability to generate sounds that vibrate through the water for miles. Any seedra can communicate with all other seedra within 10 miles, provided they are under-water.

Waves (Su): Groups of seedra are able to agitate the seas, creating huge waves and strange tides within a one-mile radius. Such effects are capable of capsizing even very large vessels when enough seedra are present, giving these creatures the power to greatly hamper sea travel if they so choose. Each seedra may only use this ability once per day. The more who use the power in a given area (within the same one-mile radius), the stronger the effects. See the table below for the maximum size of the vessel affected by this ability, the chance the vessel will be capsized for every 10 minutes it remains in the area, and the increase to all Swim DCs for those unfortunate enough to be swimming in the ocean when this power is used.

# of Seedra	Max. Size	% Capsize	Swim DC
1	Raft	30%	+2
2	Keelboat	35%	+3
3	Rowboat	40%	+4
4	Sailing Ship	45%	+5
6	Warship	55%	+6
10	Longship	60%	+8
20	Galley	65%	+10

Vassal Spirit

Medium Outsider
Hit Dice: 3d8 (13 hp)
Initiative: +0
Speed: 20 ft. (4 squares)
AC: 11 (+1 Dex), touch 11, flat-footed 11
Base Attack/Grapple: +3/+7
Attack: +3 melee (1d3)
Full Attack: Bash +3 melee (1d3)
Space/Reach: 5 ft./5 ft.
Special Attacks: Improved Grab, Chilling Presence
Special Qualities: —
Saves: Fort +3, Ref +3, Will +0
Abilities: Str 10, Dex 13, Con 10, Int 10, Wis 10, Cha 2

Skills: Craft (any three) +6, Profession (any three) +6, Handle Animal +2, Use Rope +7
Feats: Improved Grapple, Improved Unarmed Strike
Environment: Any
Organization: Solitary
Challenge Rating: 1
Treasure: None
Alignment: Always neutral
Advancement: —

A thick, flowing mass of shimmering goo flows towards you, propelling itself on translucent stalks extruded from its edges. Several sensory organs swivel toward you as it nears.

Originally summoned by a guild of architect priests, the vassal spirits were intended to provide tireless, rela-tively intelligent labor, freeing their masters to pursue more important endeavors. The Sundering simultane-ously freed the creatures and trapped them on Aryth. A few remained within the cities they had served for so long, as they were too confused and frightened to strike out on their own, but many vassal spirits simply wan-dered away from their post.

Today, vassal spirits are rarely seen. Astiraxes find them particularly satisfying prey, leading most vassal spirits to hide themselves as far from civilization as pos-sible. These creatures are able to communicate in bro-ken Trade Tongue and are always in search of work. They accept payment, but do not quote prices, and always perform whatever work is requested of them to the best of their abilities.

Combat

Vassal spirits loathe combat, though they may resort to violence to defend themselves. When they do attack, they usually use their Improved Unarmed Strike feat to hit for subdual damage with a spontaneously formed pseudopod. Alternatively, a vassal spirit may grapple in an attempt to paralyze its opponent.

Chilling Presence (Su): If the vassal spirit is able to establish a hold on its opponent, the opponent must make a DC 11 Fortitude save or suffer 1d3 points of Strength damage each round the hold is maintained. However, this attack is intensely painful for the vassal spirit, causing it 1d6 points of damage every round that it is used.

Malleable Form (Su): The vassal spirit is able to assume a vaguely humanoid shape while working, enabling it to do the same tasks as a reasonably fit human (as shown by its ability scores), and will use its skills to the utmost of its abilities while working.

Chapter Four

Animals of Eredane

Boro

Large Animal
Hit Dice: 5d8+15 (37 hp)
Initiative: +0
Speed: 40 ft.
AC: 13 (–1 size, +4 natural)
Base Attack/Grapple: +3/+11
Attack: Gore +7 melee (1d8+6)
Full Attack: Gore +7 melee (1d8+6)
Space/Reach: 10 ft./5 ft.
Special Attacks: —
Special Qualities: Scent
Saves: Fort +7, Ref +4, Will +1
Abilities: Str 18, Dex 10, Con 16, Int 2, Wis 11, Cha 5
Skills: Listen +4, Spot +4
Feats: Power Attack, Improved Bull Rush
Climate/Terrain: Central plains and southern savanna
Organization: Solitary or herd (6–30)
Challenge Rating: 2
Treasure: None
Alignment: Always neutral
Advancement: 6–7 HD (Large)

The bovine huffs cautiously at the air and, scenting no predators, continues grazing. Hundreds of the creatures dot the plains behind it.

Boros are large herd animals that roam the southern and central plains of Eredane in great numbers. Their broad bodies are covered by thick, curly hair, and two large tusks sprout from their upper jaws. They use these tusks for defense as well as to dig up the plants and roots on which they feed.

The halflings of the central plains have domesticated some boros to use as labor and pack animals, and rarely, as a food source. The orcs have driven thousands of boros up to the lands north of the Sea of Pelluria and trained them to act as mounts in combat.

Carrying Capacity: A light load for a boro is up to 300 pounds; a medium load, 301–600 pounds; a heavy load, 601–900 pounds. A boro can drag 4,500 pounds.

Grass Cat

Medium Animal
Hit Dice: 3d8+6 (19 hp)
Initiative: +8
Speed: 50 ft.
AC: 15 (+4 Dex, +1 natural)
Base Attack/Grapple: +2/+5
Attack: Bite +6 melee (1d6+3)
Full Attack: Bite +6 melee (1d6+3), 2 claws +1 melee (1d2+1)
Space/Reach: 5 ft. by 5 ft./5 ft.
Special Attacks: Trip
Special Qualities: —
Saves: Fort +5, Ref +7, Will +2
Abilities: Str 16, Dex 19, Con 15, Int 2, Wis 12, Cha 6
Skills: Hide +7, Move Silently +7
Feats: Improved Initiative, Run
Climate/Terrain: Any plains
Organization: Solitary, pair, or pack (5–12)
Challenge Rating: 1
Treasure: None
Alignment: Always neutral
Advancement: 4–5 HD (Medium)

A pair of bright eyes reflects the light of the campfire, peering in from the darkness of the plains. In the momentary glimpse as it moves away, you see a lean, feral cat padding silently through the tall grass.

Grass cats are large felines that travel in packs and hunt caribou in the northlands during the summer, migrating south during the winter to hunt boros on the central plains.

Combat

Grass cats are not aggressive by nature, but will defend their packs if they perceive a threat.

Trip (Ex): A grass cat that hits with its bite attack can attempt to trip the opponent as a free action without making a touch attack or provoking an attack of opportunity. If the attempt fails, the opponent cannot react to trip the grass cat.

Ort

Medium Animal
Hit Dice: 3d8+6 (19 hp)
Initiative: +1
Speed: 30 ft.
AC: 14 (+1 Dex, +3 natural)
Base Attack/Grapple: +2/+4
Attack: Bite +4 melee (1d6+3)
Full Attack: Bite +4 melee (1d6+3)
Space/Reach: 5 ft./5 ft.

Special Attacks: Trip
Special Qualities: Scent
Saves: Fort +5, Ref +6, Will +1
Abilities: Str 15, Dex 12, Con 14, Int 2, Wis 11, Cha 2
Skills: Listen +5, Spot +5
Feats: Alertness, Lightning Reflexes
Climate/Terrain: Any mountains or underground
Organization: Solitary, pair, or pack (5–15)
Challenge Rating: 1
Treasure: None
Alignment: Always neutral
Advancement: 4–6 HD (Medium)

Peering out of the crevice, this large rodent is covered with dark mottled hair. Its mouth is large for a creature of its size, and the teeth it contains look capable of leaving a nasty wound.

Orts are large, rodentlike omnivores that are especially common in and under the Kaladrun Mountains. They measure up to four feet in length and weigh between 60 and 100 pounds. Their long bodies are covered with short, coarse black fur that grows over their thick hides. They can be found alone, but often hunt larger prey in packs, which can be dangerous if happened upon during a hunting frenzy.

The dwarves that live underneath the Kaladruns have

Special Qualities: Scent
Saves: Fort +6, Ref +7, Will +2
Abilities: Str 21, Dex 17, Con 15, Int 2, Wis 12, Cha 6
Skills: Hide +7, Jump +9, Move Silently +11
Feats: Power Attack, Weapon Focus (claw)
Climate/Terrain: Central and southern plains
Organization: Solitary or pair
Challenge Rating: 3
Treasure: None
Alignment: Always neutral
Advancement: 6–8 HD (Large)

The grass sways, and a gigantic beast of a cat emerges. Its body ripples with muscle and its teeth are stained pink with the blood of its last meal.

Plains leopards are solitary hunters that are sometimes encountered with a mate. They are large cats that can reach seven feet in length and 350 pounds in weight. They roam the southern and central plains, stalking boros and anything else they run across. The halflings of the central plains are on constant watch for these aggressive predators, as many communities have lost townsfolk and wogrens alike to the beasts.

Combat

Plains leopards are aggressive hunters that attack smaller creatures on sight.

Pounce (Ex): If a plains leopard leaps upon a foe during the first round of combat, it can make a full attack even if it has already taken a move action.

Improved Grab (Ex): To use this ability, the plains leopard must hit with its bite attack. If it gets a hold, it can rake.

Rake (Ex): A plains leopard that gets a hold can make two rake attacks (+7 melee) with its hind legs for 1d4+2 damage each. If the plains leopard pounces on an opponent, it can also rake.

Skills: Plains leopards receive a +4 racial bonus to Hide, Jump, and Move Silently checks. In areas of tall grass or heavy undergrowth the Hide bonus improves to +12.

managed to domesticate some of these creatures, but even these tend to be easily angered and mean-spirited.

Combat

Orts are very aggressive and territorial. They do not hesitate to attack a creature that comes into their home and often prowl the mountains at night for prey.

Trip (Ex): An ort that hits with its bite attack can attempt to trip the opponent as a free action without making a touch attack or provoking an attack of opportunity. If the attempt fails, the opponent cannot react to trip the ort.

Plains Leopard

Large Animal
Hit Dice: 5d8+10 (32 hp)
Initiative: +3
Speed: 40 ft.
AC: 15 (–1 size, +3 Dex, +3 natural)
Base Attack/Grapple: +3/+12
Attack: Claws +8 melee (1d4+5)
Full Attack: 2 claws +8 melee (1d4+5), bite +2 (1d8+2)
Space/Reach: 10 ft./5 ft.
Special Attacks: Pounce, improved grab, rake 1d4+2

River Eel

Large Animal (Aquatic)
Hit Dice: 7d8+7 (38 hp)
Initiative: +2 (Dex)
Speed: Swim 60 ft. (12 squares)
AC: 15 (–1 size, +2 Dex, +4 natural)
Base Attack/Grapple: +5/+11
Attack: Bite +8 melee (1d8+4)
Full Attack: Bite +8 melee (1d8+4)
Space/Reach: 10 ft./5 ft.
Special Attacks: Improved grab
Saves: Fort +5, Ref +7, Will +2

Abilities: Str 17, Dex 15, Con 13, Int 2, Wis 12, Cha 2

Skills: Listen +8, Spot +8

Feats: Alertness, Diehard, Endurance

Climate/Terrain: Any river

Organization: Solitary, pair, or school (3–6)

Challenge Rating: 2

Treasure: None

Alignment: Always neutral

Advancement: 8–12 HD (Large); 13–18 (Huge)

A long, toothy jaw emerges from the river. Beneath the water you can see the reptile's vestigial front legs and the slashing of its long flat tail.

River eels are long, aquatic reptiles that hunt their prey in the rivers across Eredane; they flop about when on land and are only a threat in the water. The greatest of these creatures can reach 20 feet long and top 2,000 pounds, though most are only half this size.

Combat

River eels are aggressive hunters that have been known to topple small rafts and boats, devouring those inside as they try to swim to safety. Otherwise, they attack single opponents until they get a hold and then swim away to safely devour their prey.

Improved Grab (Ex): To use this ability, the river eel must hit with its bite attack. If it gets a hold, it deals automatic bite damage each round that the hold is maintained.

Sea Dragon

Huge Animal (Aquatic)

Hit Dice: 12d8+84 (138 hp)

Initiative: +1

Speed: Swim 40 ft. (8 squares)

AC: 16 (–4 size, +1 Dex, +9 natural)

Base Attack/Grapple: +9/+25

Attack: Bite +18 melee (3d6+8/19–20/x2)

Full Attack: Bite +18 melee (3d6+8/19–20/x2) and tail slap +12 melee (1d8+4)

Space/Reach: 20 ft./10 ft.

Special Attacks: Improved grab, swallow whole

Special Qualities: Blindsight 100 ft.

Saves: Fort +15, Ref +9, Will +6

Abilities: Str 26, Dex 13, Con 24, Int 2, Wis 14, Cha 6

Skills: Listen +9, Spot +10

Feats: Improved Bull Rush, Improved Critical (bite), Improved Natural Attack (bite), Power Attack, Weapon Focus (bite)

Climate/Terrain: Any aquatic

Organization: Solitary

Challenge Rating: 8

Treasure: None

Alignment: Always neutral

Advancement: 13–24 HD (Gargantuan); 24–36 (Colossal)

This goliath sea creature's long, thin body is dwarfed by the unhinging jaws at its head.

Combat

Sea dragons attempt to swallow one opponent at a time, while using their massive tails to whip other opponents and drive them away.

Improved Grab (Ex): To use this ability, the sea dragon must hit with its bite attack. If it gets a hold, it deals automatic bite damage and can attempt to swallow the opponent.

Swallow Whole (Ex): A sea dragon can try to swallow a grabbed opponent of Large or smaller size by making a successful grapple check. Once inside, the opponent takes 3d6+8 points of crushing damage per round from the creature's muscular gullet. A swallowed creature can cut its way out by using a Tiny or Small slashing weapon to deal 25 points of damage to the sea dragon's gut (AC 16). Once the creature exits, muscular action closes the hole; another swallowed opponent must cut its own way out. The sea dragon's interior can hold 2 Large, 8 Medium, 32 Small, or 128 Tiny or smaller opponents.

Chapter Five

Agents of Shadow

Ceelian Asale

Female Miransil Exp9: CR 8; Medium Humanoid (4 ft. 7 in. tall); HD 9d6+36; hp 70; Init +1; Spd 30 ft (6 squares); AC 11 (+1 Dex); Base Atk +6; Grp +7; Atks +7/+2 melee (longspear 1d8+2); SQ +5 feet swim as move-equiv, +10 ft. swim as full-round, +2 bonus against Enchantment spells or effects, hold breath for 6x Con score in rounds, low-light vision, proficient in longspear, javelin, longbow, and shortbow, exotic elven weapons as martial weapons, 2 extra points of spell energy, 2 0-level spells 1/day if Cha is 10+; AL NG; SV Fort +7, Ref +3, Will +5; Str 13, Dex 11, Con 18, Int 14, Wis 9, Cha 17.

Skills: Appraise +17, Climb +10 (+14 in trees), Escape Artist +12, Knowledge (history) +14, Knowledge (Miraleen) +14, Search +15, Swim +20, Tumble +8, Use Rope +8.

Feats: Endurance, Great Fortitude, Skill Focus (Appraise), Skill Focus (Swim).

Languagues: High Elven, Jungle Mouth, Trader's Tongue.

Possessions: sari, longspear, diving bladder (holds one full breath of air), minor charms (select 1d4 minor charms), dagger, *circlet of persuasion*.

The diminutive elven woman looks boldly into your eyes, a captivating smile dancing across her lips. Her voice reaches out to you, making music as she speaks.

Ceelian is one of the greatest divers among the Miransil, able to stay underwater for more than twenty minutes at a stretch when using a diving bladder. She also has an uncanny knack for finding the best spots for artifacts and treasure during dive-hunts. Her glossy black hair and indigo eyes give her an exotic look, enhanced by the confidence she has gained over a hundred successful dives.

Her success comes partially from her amazing physical prowess, and partially from the intense research she does before every dive. She spends months preparing for each dive, studying records of the previous years' dives and talking with the oldest living elves. This research allows her to identify prime areas and make important decisions before she slips under the waves, saving precious seconds underwater.

As a local celebrity in Alloduan, Ceelian attracts a

great deal of attention from the local unmarried men. Her kind heart prevents her from firmly dissuading any of them, but in truth she has no interest in being anything other than a friend to all she meets. Only the sea and the thrill of finding a place unseen by fey for thousands of years stir the passions of her heart.

During one of last season's dive-hunts, Ceelian found herself in more trouble than she bargained for. Deep underwater, in a newly discovered section of ruin, she encountered a demonling named Asale. Her search for artifacts accidentally broke the spell containing the creature. It used what little magical energy it could muster to pull down the unstable ceiling, trapping her within the chamber. After she passed out, but before she had completely drowned, Asale possessed the helpless elf and swam to the surface.

Asale was once a mighty creature, a free-willed demon that wreaked havoc among the elder fey that populated the now-submerged city under the waves. They trapped him with mighty magics, ripping his essence from his body and entrapping it in a sacred vessel. When Ceelian released him, the demond intended to kill the woman and feast on her spirit . . . instead, he found that he could quite easily take her body as his own. He revels in his newfound freedom, but fears what would happen if he is revealed. For now he is content to sit quietly below the surface of Ceelian's personality, emerging only occasionally to create discord by tempting and manipulating her many suitors. So far he has arranged for two of them to meet gruesome deaths by giving them tasks to "impress" his beautiful host.

The demon also fears that the Shadow will one day learn of his existence. The two were not on friendly terms before the Sundering. If discovered, Asale will drag his host back to the City of the Sea, hoping against hope to find a way to return to his infernal home.

Possessed Ceelian

While Asale is active, Ceelian gains the fiendish template. This template gives her the following special abilities: smite good (1/day, +9 damage), darkvision 60 ft., cold and fire resistance 10, damage reduction 5/magic, and spell resistance 14. Her CR increases to 10 and her alignment changes to chaotic evil. She also gains the following skills: Bluff +18, Diplomacy +18, Intimidate +18, Knowledge (arcana) +16, Knowledge (religion) +16, Sense Motive +14.

The infernal transformation also causes a number of minute physical changes. Her figure becomes lush, while her hair lengthens slightly and becomes a wild tangle. Her violet eyes radiate faint light. Her lips become dark red, as do her finger and toenails. Ceelian does not remember anything she says or does while possessed. Her periodic blackouts are beginning to worry her. As the seasonal dive-hunts approach, she has begun to realize that she may not be able to participate unless she can find a cure.

Darshod of the Dead Mother Tribe

Male Orc Chr17 (charismatic): CR 17; Medium Humanoid (6 ft. 2 in. tall); HD 17d6+17; hp 79; Init +3; Spd 30 ft.; AC 22 (+3 Dex, *robe of the archmagi, ring of protection +4*); Base Atk +12; Grp +11; Atks +11/+6/+1 ranged (1d4–1, dagger); SQ +1 racial bonus on damage rolls against dwarves, +2 racial bonus to saves vs. spells, +2 racial bonus on Survival and Intimidate checks, +2 on caster level checks to overcome SR, art of magic, cold resistance 5, darkvision 60 ft., force of personality, group combat bonus, light sensitivity, night fighting, proficient with vardatch, spells, SR 18, summon familiar; AL LE; SV Fort +10, Ref +9, Will +16; Str 9, Dex 11, Con 12, Int 12, Wis 15, Cha 22.

Skills: Alchemy +20, Concentration +20, Craft (jewelry) +20, Diplomacy +15, Intimidate +23, Knowledge (arcane) +20, Knowledge (nature) +16, Scry +21, Spellcraft +21.

Feats: Empower Spell, Extend Spell, Quicken Spell, Silent Spell, Still Spell; Magecraft, Spell Focus (Necromancy), Craft Spell Talisman; Craft Greater Spell Talisman; Spellcasting (Abjuration), Spellcasting (Divination), Spellcasting (Enchantment), Spellcasting (Illusion), Spellcasting (Lesser Conjuration), Greater Spellcasting (Greater Conjuration), Spellcasting

(Necromancy), Spellcasting (Transmutation), Spellcasting (Universal).

Spells Known (23 points of spell energy/day; DC 16 + spell level): 0—*arcane mark, cure minor wounds, create water, detect magic, know direction, mage hand, open/close, prestidigitation, ray of frost, resistance*; 1st—*charm person, comprehend languages, cause fear*, hypnotism, mage armor, mount, obscuring mist, ray of enfeeblement*, shield*; 2nd—*acid arrow, animal messenger, blindness/deafness*, detect good, detect thoughts, enthrall, fog cloud, ghoul touch*, protection from arrows, see invisibility, summon swarm, undetectable alignment, web, warp wood*; 3rd—*clairaudience/clairvoyance, cure serious wounds, dispel magic, flame arrow, gaseous form, meld into stone, neutralize poison, poison*, secret page, slow, summon monster III, tongues, water breathing*; 4th—*black tentacles, contagion*, locate creature, minor globe of invulnerability, polymorph self, scrying, stoneskin, summon monster IV*; 5th—*animate dead, break enchantment, cloudkill, magic jar*, prying eyes, summon monster V, telepathic bond, wall of iron*; 6th—*analyze dweomer, fire seeds, flesh to stone, globe of invulnerability, greater dispelling, guards and wards, shades, stone to flesh, summon monster VI, true seeing*; 7th—*finger of death*, greater scrying, heal, power word stun, spell turning, summon monster VII, wind walk*; 8th—*clone, discern location, create greater undead, mass charm, power word blind, trap the soul**, 9th—*elemental swarm, energy drain*, power word kill, refuge*.

* Necromancy spells. Save DC 17 + spell level.

Rituals: animate dead, clone, create greater undead, elemental swarm, greater scrying, locate creature, mass charm, scrying, summon monster VI, summon monster VII, tongues

Possessions: greater spell talisman (necromancy), great spell talisman (lesser conjuration), true charm necklace (gives wearer the benefit of the *sanctuary* spell during surprise rounds), *carpet of flying, cloak of charisma +2, ring of protection +4, robe of the archmagi (black), wand of cure critical wounds,* 1–6 scrolls of each level.

Ginnuin, Imp Familiar Rog5: CR 7; Tiny Outsider; HD 3d8+5d6; hp 39; Init +7; Spd 20 ft., fly 50 ft. (perfect); AC 25 (+2 size, +4 Dex, +5 natural, +4 *mage armor*); Base Atk +3; Grp –5; Atks +11 melee (1d4 plus poison, sting); Space/Reach: 2½ ft./0 ft.; SA poison, spell-like abilities, sneak attack +3d6; SQ Alternate form, damage reduction 5/good or silver, darkvision 60 ft., fast healing 2, immunity to poison, resistance to fire 5, trapfinding, improved evasion, trap sense +1, uncanny dodge, share spells, empathic link, deliver touch spells, speak with master, SR 22, free scry by Darshod 1/day; AL LE; SV Fort +4, Ref +12, Will +5; Str 10, Dex 18, Con 10, Int 10, Wis 12, Cha 14.

Skills: Alchemy +20, Bluff +10, Concentration +20, Craft (jewelry) +20, Diplomacy +11, Disable Device +12, Hide +20, Intimidate +23, Knowledge (arcane) +20, Knowledge (nature) +16, Knowledge (Night Kings) +6, Listen +12, Move Silently +16, Open Lock +12, Scry +21, Search +11, Sense Motive +10, Sleight of Hand +12, Spellcraft +20, Spot +12, Survival +4 (+6 following tracks).

Feats: Dodge, Improved Feint, Improved Initiative, Weapon Finesse (sting).

Languages: Write and read all: Black Tongue, Courtier, Erenlander, Gnomish, High Elven Pidgin, Norther, Old Dwarven Pidgin, Orcish, Trader Tongue.

Poison (Ex): Injury, Fortitude DC 13, initial damage 1d4 Dex, secondary damage 2d4 Dex. The save DC is Constitution-based and includes a +2 racial bonus.

Spell-Like Abilities: At will—*detect good, detect magic, invisibility* (self only); 1/day—*suggestion* (DC 15). Caster level 6th. The save DC is Charisma-based. 1/week—*commune* to ask six questions (caster level 12).

Alternate Form (Su): May *polymorph* into a bat or monstrous spider at will (caster level 12).

Possessions: potion of clairaudience/clairvoyance, potion of gaseous form, potion of stoneskin.

The light cringes away from the tall, thin orcish figure before you. His wild eyes gleam within the shrunken coal-black skull of his face. Blood red robes embroidered with blasphemous sigils drape a frame meant to carry muscle but somehow withered. As his lips part, the air shudders under the foul power of the mystical words pouring forth.

They say that when Darshod clawed his way out of his dead mother's womb, he screamed blasphemous words so vile that even his legate midwife turned pale. The stories do not do the truth justice; Darshod not only killed his mother but also sucked the soul out of his midwife. When the chaos cleared, the *kurasatch udareen* commanded that the child be taken to Theros Obsidia. She rightly believed that a creature with such native arcane power could only be controlled by the most powerful of legates.

Upon his arrival at Theros Obsidia, the legates tested the child for magical potential. The first legate to attempt the test died. The second, more careful than his predecessor, determined that Darshod engaged in a special relationship with Izrador. Although trapped in the body of a child, his soul was somehow old and already deeply trained in the arts of arcane power. The legates helped the child remember and translate his powers, rather than indoctrinating him into their order. The truth, which Darshod has revealed to none, is that his soul is indeed old. His father was a talented channeler who died just after fathering the child on an orcish whore. In his final moments, the father called upon the Shadow to save him. The dark god did so, transplanting the soul into the waiting child held in the mother's womb. For the next nine months, Izador whispered blasphemies into the child's mind.

In time, Darshod became what Izrador made him to be: the perfect assistant to the Night King Ardherin. He serves willingly, lending his arcane might to the chosen of his god. He also strikes hard into the heart of the Order of Shadow, keeping them in line and under heel as much as possible.

Underneath his loyal service, Darshod watches and waits. He watches his master Ardherin most closely of all, waiting for a time when the Night King will slip. Darshod believes he knows a way to transfer his soul into the Night King's body, taking the elf's nearly limitless arcane might for himself. He also believes that so long as the assault on the elves does not falter, Izrador will ignore the switch. Whether Darshod's belief proves true in practice remains to be seen, but he hopes to find out soon.

Gorgathan of the Mother of Bone Tribe

Male Orc Bar4/Lgt9: CR 13; Medium Humanoid (6 ft. 5 in. tall); HD 4d12+9d8+26; hp 99; Init +1; Spd 30 ft (6 squares); AC 21 (–1 Dex, +9 half plate w. extended *magic vestment,* +3 buckler w. extended *magic vestment*); Base Atk +10; Grp +15; Atk: +17/+12 melee (1d8+7, longsword w. extended *greater magic weapon*) or +9 ranged (1d10, heavy crossbow); SA spells; SQ +1 racial bonus on damage rolls against dwarves, +2 racial bonus to saves vs. spells, +2 racial bonus on Survival and Intimidate checks, astirax companion, cold resistance 5, darkvision 60 ft., domain abilities, group combat bonus, light sensitivity, night fighting, proficient with vardatch, rage 2/day, rebuke undead, uncanny dodge; AL NE; SV Fort +15, Ref +6, Will +13; Str 20, Dex 8, Con 14, Int 12, Wis 17, Cha 12.

Skills: Climb +9, Concentration +11, Handle Animal +8, Intimidate +10, Jump +6, Knowledge (religion) +10, Listen +6, Spellcraft +9, Spot +8, Survival +8

Feats: Combat Casting, Extend Spell, Iron Will, Power Attack, Track, Weapon Focus (long sword), Weapon Proficiency (long sword).

Languages: Write and read all: Black Tongue, Courtier, Erenlander, High Elven Pidgin, Old Dwarven Pidgin, Orcish, Trader Tongue.

Domains: Destruction (1/day smite adds +4 attack and +9 damage, declared before attack), War.

Spells Prepared (6, 5+1, 5+1, 4+1, 3+1, 1+1; base DC = 13 + spell level): 0—*cure minor wounds (3), detect poison, purify food and drink, resistance;* 1st—*command, cure light wounds, divine favor (2), protection from good, shield of faith;* 2nd—*cure moderate wounds (2), hold person, shatter (2), spiritual weapon;* 3rd—*bestow curse, contagion, cure serious wounds, protection from elements, wind wall;* 4th—*divine power,* extended *magic vestment (2), spell immunity;* 5th— extended *greater magic weapon, righteous might.*

Possessions: Masterwork longsword, masterwork half-plate armor, masterwork buckler, *cloak of resistance +3, dust of appearance, gauntlets of ogre power, necklace of fireballs (Type V), periapt of wisdom +2, potion of cure moderate wounds (2), potion of protection from arrows 10/magic.*

The orc before you unleashes an ear-splitting war cry tainted with equal parts rage, hate, and anguish. His scarred half plate armor gives off metallic shrieks as he charges forward, longsword raised high.

As a child, Gorgathan dreamed of great things. He knew that the Shadow had special plans for him, plans that would elevate him beyond the brutal struggle of the common herd. His conviction won him no friends as a child. Isolated even by orcish standards, he became the focus of the budding rage of his tribe's children. When the time came for him to march into battle, they put him in front, hoping that he would go down under a hail of elven arrows, never to bother them again.

The Shadow protected him that day. In the months that followed, the young Gorgathan went through the hell known as the Caraheen, watching his youthful tormenters die around him one by one. When he finally felt the call to join his brother legates, he went with a light heart and happy memories.

At Theros Obsidia, the newly made legate discov-

ly and quietly to himself. He knows that Izrador will watch over him and bring him his destiny.

Grial the Fey Killer

Male Orc Bar4/Ftr 16: CR 20; Medium Humanoid (6ft. 8 in. tall); HD 4d12+16d10+80; hp 203; Init +7; Spd 40 ft (8 squares); AC 29 (+3 Dex, +4 *breastplate, amulet of natural armor +4, ring of protection +3*); Base Atk +20; Grp +28; Atks +27/+27/+22/+17/+12 melee (1d12+9+2d6 vs. elves, *+1 speed elfbane vardatch*) and +28/+23 melee (1d6+6, *+2 returning mithril urutuk hatchet*), or +23/+18/+13/+8 ranged (1d8+4, composite longbow [+4 Str]); SQ +1 racial bonus on damage rolls against dwarves, +2 racial bonus to saves vs. spells, +2 racial bonus on Survival and Intimidate checks, cold resistance 5, darkvision 60 ft, fast movement, group combat bonus, light sensitivity, nightfighting, proficient with vardatch, rage 2/day, uncanny dodge, fire resistance 10, DR 5/magic; AL LN; SV Fort +19, Ref +9, Will +9; Str 26, Dex 17, Con 18, Int 14, Wis 16, Cha 14.

Skills: Climb +15, Intimidate +11, Jump +14, Knowledge (geography) +10, Knowledge (history) +10, Knowledge (warfare) +10, Listen +10, Profession (soldier) +14, Ride +12, Spot +8, Survival +12.

Feats: Blind-Fight, Cleave, Combat Expertise, Combat Reflexes, Dodge, Great Cleave, Improved Initiative, Improved Sunder, Improved Trip, Improved Two-Weapon Fighting, Improved Unarmed Attack, Mobility, Power Attack, Quick Draw, Spring Attack, Two-Weapon Fighting.

Languages: Write and read all: Black Tongue, Old Dwarven Pidgin, High Elven Pidgin, Orcish, Trader Tongue, Erenlander, Norther.

Possessions: +4 fire resistant invulnerability breast-plate, +1 speed elfbane vardatch, +2 returning mithril urutuk hatchet, greataxe, buckler, 4 daggers, composite longbow (+4 Str), 40 arrows, *potion of heal (3), belt of giant strength (+4), amulet of natural armor +4, Fist of the North* (covenant item), *ring of protection +3, ring of freedom of movement.*

The grizzled orc pierces you with a level gaze. His eyes hold none of the madness and rage associated with his kin, just a calm certainty and careful measuring. In a moment you feel yourself weighted in the scales of his mind . . . then casually set aside as though the entire measure of your life represents nothing more than a minor annoyance.

No signs or portents heralded Grial's birth. Born in anonymity among the hordes of orcs in the far north, he trained like the rest of his tribe. He seemed no different from his cousins: He hated the fey, barely tolerated his family and comrades, and seethed with the rage bequeathed to him at birth.

ered the depths of folly of his childhood yearnings. Treated as little more than a servant, the proud orc warrior learned to bend his neck to humans and others who strode the halls. He tended candles and waxed the floors, learning the dark rituals by following on the heels of those who practiced them. At night his dreams showed him vistas of unimaginable power and splendor, but the dawn always rose to find him bedded down in a bare novitiate's cell.

Finally, after a decade of service and proving his worth, Gorgathan the warrior legate received his great assignment. He joined the army of the legendary Grial the Fey Killer. When the majority of the Fey Killer's other legates were slaughtered in an ambush by halfling wogren riders, Gorgathan became his chief legate advisor.

Unfortunately, Grial neither wants nor needs his help. Gorgathan is more ignored and abandoned now than he ever was back at Theros Obsidia, or even in the great camps of his tribe. At least in those dark places, people cared enough to make him miserable. Grial considers him completely irrelevant. Yet still the dreams come.

Every dusk, Gorgathan prays to Izrador to bless his blade and keep harm from him. Then he walks alone into the darkness, seeking to find that one great kill that will raise him to his superiors' notice. He searches for the strongest heroes and mightiest channelers of the elves. Stalking in the night, Gorgathan mutters feverish-

All of that changed during his first battle. After the initial charge against the elven defenses at dusk, over half of his company lay dead. Rather than being swept up into a haze of rage, Grial mentally stepped back to assess the situation. With cold logic and steely resolve, he shouted his way to the top of the remaining command structure. Within 10 minutes, he had rallied the troops. Within 30, he had ordered a strategic withdraw with harrying forces to cover the retreat. By midnight, he led his decimated company to victory, turning loose his rested but enraged forces against the weary elves.

In bloody victory after bloody victory, Grial led his troops from the front, displaying a tactical and strategic genius unrivaled in Ayrth. He committed atrocities against the fey that even now leave those who hear of them pale and shaking, but he always did so with one goal in mind: to win the war. Each mutilation or maiming was a carefully considered blow against the enemy's spirit and a boost to his troops' morale. Through it all he walked and watched, fought and murdered, without losing his head. He came to regard the poisonous rage in his blood as a weakness that the fey could exploit, so he strove though discipline to bring it under control.

As the young orc rose to prominence, Izrador granted him a special boon. The Order of Shadow gave him access to ancient books of history and warfare penned by the Sarcosans and brought with them from across the sea. From them, he learned logistics, strategy, and tactics. He also gained a sense of the shape of history itself, and knows that in these end days there is little hope for anyone. The futile victory over the elves will save no one but Izrador.

Now Grial leads the battle against Erethor with brutal practicality. He measures victories in the old way, weighing lives, resources, and time against possible gain. The elves, long adapted to the blind charges of the orcs, cannot understand this careful, canny orcish general. The legates secretly question his loyalty, believing that effectiveness cannot replace blind devotion. Yet none can deny that Grial's unconventional tactics and willingness to withdraw forces and let the fey go occasionally unmolested have done more for the war than a hundred years of unrelenting waves of mindless death.

Grial has become the vision of an old soldier, a weary general who fights on because he does not know any other way. Other orcs fear him, knowing that there is something in his soul they cannot understand. Even the oruks regard him with an almost mystical terror. They recognize genius when they see it.

Fist of the North

This dark iron amulet has a black star sapphire set in its center. The metal of the amulet is always cold, the twists and turns of the filigree sometimes coating with frost for no detectable reason. Anyone wearing the *fist* takes 1 point of cold damage every round.

No one knows where it came from, but the Order of Shadow gave the *fist* to Grial after a particularly bloody battle in which he oversaw the destruction of a nigh-impregnable dwarven citadel. At the time, he just shrugged and went back to the killing.

The *fist of the north* grants the following powers:

3rd level—Wearer gains the Improved Unarmed Strike feat.

4th level—Once per day the wearer may cast *cure moderate wounds* as a 5th level caster.

9th level—Wearer gains a +4 on opposed rolls when bull rushing, disarming, grappling, overrunning, or tripping.

12th level—Wearer may communicate telepathically with all allies within 1 mile as a free action.

Shealgruf One-Arm

Male Orc Rog1/Bar13: CR 14; Medium Humanoid (7 ft. 3 in. tall); HD 13d12+1d6+42; hp 133; Init +5; Spd 30 ft. (8 squares); AC 23 (+1 Dex, *+3 glamered banded mail, ring of protection +1, ring of force shield*); Base Atk +13; Grp +19; Atks +20/+15/+10 melee (1d12+7/17-20/x2, *+1 keen vardatch*) or +14 ranged (1d6+6, javelin); SA +1d6 sneak attack; SQ +1 racial bonus on damage rolls against dwarves, +2 racial bonus to saves vs. spells, +2 racial bonus on Survival and Intimidate checks, cold resistance 5, damage reduction 3/—, darkvision 60 ft., fast movement, greater rage 4/day, group combat bonus, improved uncanny dodge, light sensitivity, nightfighting, proficient with vardatch, trap sense +4, uncanny dodge; AL CE; SV Fort +11, Ref +7, Will +7; Str 23, Dex 13, Con 17, Int 10, Wis 13, Cha 15.

Skills: Bluff +10, Climb +22, Intimidate +18, Jump +22, Perform (storytelling) +10.

Feats: Cleave, Great Cleave, Improved Initiative, Leadership, Power Attack.

Languages (spoken only)*:* Black Tongue, Old Dwarven Pidgin, High Elven Pidgin, Orcish.

Possessions: +1 keen vardatch, masterwork battleaxe, 6 javelins, 2 daggers, *+3 glamered banded mail, ring of force shield, ring of protection +1, potion of cure moderate wounds (2)*.

The one-armed orc before you swells as his skin reddens and ropy veins writhe under his skin. White foam flecked with dark red blood falls from his mouth, chiseled teeth cutting at his lips as he screams for your deaths.

Shealgruf is a legend, an orcish warrior standing over seven feet tall and weighing in at over 300 lbs. Over the years since he lost his right arm in battle, his left has become massively developed. His burned and scarred face frames smoldering red eyes, a feature he uses in battle.

Shealgruf is arguably the best-known member of the orcish legions, a larger-than-life figure that seemingly sprang out of nowhere. He appeared at the side of the Night King Jahzir twenty years ago, a roaring figure that could cut down any who opposed him. He travels though the countryside surrounded by his devoted following, hunting down rebels and finding new slaves for the war machine.

In the absence of truth, rumors and legends gather around Shealgruf like flies to a corpse. It is rumored that he cut his own arm off rather than be taken prisoner when an elven spell bound him to a tree. They say that he eats a fresh halfling every day for dinner, can leap a quarter of a mile from a standing start, and breathes fire on his enemies. Tales claim that he choked an oruk captain to death while the oruk smote him with 20 blows from his vardatch, and walked away without a scratch.

Some of these stories are true; enough of them that his underlings obey him without question. The rest have sprung up through a combination of everyday tale-telling and subtle plants by Shealgruf himself. While not one for intellectual discourse, the orc is clever, and knows that when the stories begin to falter, his enemies will see that his aging body has begun to do so as well.

Shealgruf leads his troops with a mixture of terror and devotion unmatched by any commander in Aryth. He is second only to Jahzir himself in commanding the loyalty of his troops. He also relies heavily on the Night King's advice, combining practical military knowledge with sheer bloody-minded determination. Jahzir treats Shealgruf almost like a pet, holding him up as an example of what a good orc should be.

This formidable warrior retains the respect of his closest cadre of warriors by leading them into battle personally. Ironically, this allows him to avoid having to do much of the killing or dying, as any would-be challengers find themselves struck down by one of the "elite" orcs who hunt by his side. These orcs believe Shealgruf to be divinely inspired, the greatest orc who has ever or shall ever live. Anyone who dares to challenge this belief, they say, must be made to pay dearly.

Purlan Marrick

Male Gnome Rog5/Insurgent Spy 6: CR 11; Small Humanoid (3 ft. 4 in. tall); HD 11d6+11; hp 52; Init +7; Spd 20 ft.; AC 17 (+1 size, +3 Dex, *+1 studded leather*); Base Atk +7; Grp +3; Atk +11 melee (1d4, masterwork dagger) or +11 ranged (1d8, masterwork folding light crossbow); SA +2 on saves against spells and spell-like effects; conceal magic, evasion, shadow contacts (incredible), shadow speak +3, sneak attack +5d6, trapfinding, uncanny dodge; SQ gnome traits; AL CE; SV Fort +5, Ref +12, Will +4; Str 10, Dex 16, Con 13, Int 15, Wis 12, Cha 17.

Skills: Appraise +7*, Bluff +19*[†], Decipher Script +11, Diplomacy +15*, Disguise +16, Forgery +12[†],

Gather Information +14†, Hide +11, Listen +14, Knowledge (Eren River Valley) +9, Move Silently +23, Perform +5, Profession (boater and sailor) +9*, Search +12, Sense Motive +14, Sleight of Hand +10, Swim +8, Use Rope +4, Survival +1‡.

Feats: Inconspicuous, Improved Initiative, Skill Focus (bluff), Weapon Finesse (dagger).

Languages: Black Tongue, Erenlander, High Elven Pidgin, Orcish, Old Dwarven Pidgin, Trader's Tongue.

Possessions: +1 studded leather armor, masterwork dagger, drop sheathe, masterwork folding light crossbow, 10 bolts, *ring of mind shielding, boots of elvenkind, stone of alarm,* one pair of hollow-heeled boots holding a *potion of cure moderate wounds* and a vial of orcbane.

* In addition, Purlan Marrick gains a +4 racial bonus to these skills when made during trading activities.

† In addition, Purlan Marrick gains a +4 racial bonus to these skills when made during smuggling activities.

‡ +4 when on rivers.

Purlan Marrick was trained in the shipping trade by his father, Bresbin, who owned the Hard Rain Trading Company. Bresbin kept the business small, so as not to draw attention to his smuggling operations. Purlan grew up resenting the man for foregoing larger, more lucrative jobs, while his family went hungry. Shortly after Purlan came of age, Bresbin was caught running weapons and was immediately put to death. Purlan inherited the business and vowed not to make his father's mistakes. However, since his father was a known resistance smuggler, Purlan found "honest" work hard to come by. To his disgust, he was forced to smuggle weapons and healing supplies for several resistance groups, simply because no reputable work came his way. Purlan did his job well and made a small reputation for himself among the insurgents, all the while cursing them.

While smuggling a fugitive past a garrison near occupied Erenhead, Purlan realized that he was sitting on an opportunity. He leaked word of the criminal's presence to a local legate. The next night, under cover of darkness, the legate and his orc inspection party apprehended the fugitive on Purlan's barge. The legate ordered the fugitive slain and set the vessel afire. As for Purlan, he was brought before the Night King Sunulael, and offered the opportunity to serve as a set of eyes and ears for the Shadow along the Eren River. Purlan accepted, and set about rebuilding his family's trading company into an unknowing network of spies, all reporting to him. Capitalizing on his reputation among the free races as a trusted smuggler, Purlan is able to gather information of insurgent activities throughout southern Erenland, and then relay the information to his contacts among the Order of Shadow.

Only a few have so far discovered the treachery of Purlan Marrick and the truth behind the Hard Rain Trading Company, but those who could not be bought off have been imprisoned or slain outright by Purlan's new allies.

Zebrim the Slayer

Male Sarcosan Rog12: CR 12; Medium Humanoid (5 ft., 3 in. tall); HD 12d6+24; hp 69; Init +9; Spd 30 ft; AC 20 (+5 Dex, *studded leather of shadow +1*, +1 masterwork buckler); Base Atk +9; Grp +11; Atks +15/+10 melee (1d6+2/17–20/x2, masterwork ceduku) or +14/+9 melee (1d6+2, scimitar) or +16/+11 ranged (1d6+2, masterwork composite shortbow [+2 Str]); SQ +1 racial bonus on Reflex saves, +4 racial bonus on Handle Animals and Ride checks (horses only), +1 racial bonus on weapon damage rolls when attacking from horseback, +2 racial bonus on Bluff, Diplomacy, and Sense Motive checks, +2 racial bonus on Survival and Gather Information checks in southern Erenland, improved uncanny dodge, Knowledge (southern Erenland) is a class skill, natural horseman, opportunist, proficient with cedeku, sneak attack +6d6, trapfinding, trap sense +3, uncanny dodge; AL CE; SV Fort +6, Ref +14, Will +4; Str 14, Dex 20, Con 15, Int 18, Wis 10, Cha 16.

Skills: Balance +17, Bluff +17, Decipher Script +18, Escape Artist +14, Gather Information +15, Hide +31, Intimidate +15, Jump +18, Knowledge (southern erenland) +18, Listen +14, Move Silently +15, Perform +8, Profession (jester) +3, Ride +16, Search +18, Sense Motive +16, Sleight of Hand +14, Spot +15, Survival +9, Tumble +17, Use Rope +10.

Feats: Combat Expertise, Improved Critical

(cedeku), Improved Disarm, Improved Feint, Improved Initiative, Track.

Possessions: masterwork ceduku, scimitar, 2 daggers, masterwork composite shortbow (+2 Str), *+1 seeking arrows (20)*, *+2 flame arrows (10)*, masterwork arrows (20), *+1 studded leather armor of shadow*, masterwork buckler, *ring of chameleon power, potion of blur, potion of cure serious wounds, potion of darkvision, potion of invisibility, potion of spider climb*, pouch full of slender finger bones.

The pale tan skin of the sarcosan racing towards you has a disturbing, mottled look. His watery black eyes blaze with fury as he screams a foul epitaph upon you and all of your descendants.

Zebrim stands just less than five and a half feet tall, although he wears slightly elevated boots to push him over that threshold. He wears loose, flowing, dun colored robes over his studded leather armor. Strips of human skin bind back his long black hair, allowing him to move freely in combat. His unusually light skin is the result of several layers of erotic and sadomasochistic bleached tattoos tracing over the majority of his body. He never speaks about how he got them, but has been known to rattle his pouch of finger bones when questioned.

This twisted man grew up as a foundling in the court of one of the petty princes. He was raised by a whore and a collaborator, and their lives of deception and selfishness shaped his view of the world. His early years were spent as a court jester and occasional clown, tormented by cruel jokes. In time, his cunning and vicious nature allowed him to achieve some rank in the courts. When he finally came of age, his foster mother and father both vanished mysteriously.

After years of service, Zebrim finally received horse rights from his lord. Unfortunately, it turned out that he had no aptitude at all for horsemanship. He killed his first horse out of spite. His second proved no more responsive, so he broke its legs and beat it to death. Since that time, he has ridden no single mount for more than a week.

The court legates took notice of Zebrim's sadism, and approached him with an offer. They needed someone to hunt down freedom fighters. In return, they would supply him with an endless supply of fresh slaves to satisfy his appetites. Zebrim agreed. Now he leads the most bloodthirsty band of killers to ride the plains, the *Carasoom.* For every Sarcosan freerider he brings in, he and his men receive "body rights" to a fresh slave. While even some legates find the results of this bargain disturbing, they cannot deny its effectiveness.

Over the past year, Zebrim has become angry with Kalif Saida's skill at evading capture; that cleverness has cut into Zebrim's own pleasures. Worse, the legates have threatened to not only not reward, but punish him as well if the Kalif is not captured soon. It is slowly occurring to this madman that perhaps, just perhaps, he does not control his own life.

Sample Legates

Lesser Legate

Male Erenlander Lgt1: CR 1; Medium Humanoid (5 ft. 11 in. tall); HD 1d8+5; hp 13; Init +0; Spd 20 ft.; AC 17 (+0 Dex, +6 splint mail, +1 small wooden shield); Base Atk +0; Grp +0; Atk +0 melee (1d8, heavy mace) or +0 ranged (1d8, light crossbow); Space/Reach 5 ft./5ft.; SA rebuke undead, spells; AL NE; SV Fort +4, Ref +0, Will +7; Str 10, Dex 10, Con 14, Int 10, Wis 17, Cha 13.

Skills: Concentration +4 (+8), Diplomacy +3, Heal +5, Intimidate +4, Knowledge (central Erenland) +0, Knowledge (religion) +4, Profession (record keeper) +7, Spellcraft +3.

Feats: Combat Casting, Iron Will, Scribe Scroll.

Languages: Black Tongue, Erenlander.

Spells Prepared (3/2+1; base DC = 13 + spell level; domains: evil and magic): 0—*detect magic, detect poison, read magic;* 1st—*cause fear, cure light wounds, protection from good*.*

* Indicates a domain spell.

Possessions: splint mail, heavy mace, light crossbow, 10 bolts, small wooden shield, scroll of *shield of faith*, scroll of *command*, 20 gp.

Soldier Legate

Male Dorn Lgt4: CR 4; Medium Humanoid (6 ft. 5 in. tall); HD 4d8+4; hp 25; Init +4; Spd 20 ft.; AC 20 (+0 Dex, +8 full plate, +2 large steel shield); Base Atk +3; Grp +6; Atk +8 melee (1d8+3, masterwork longsword) or +3 ranged (1d10, heavy crossbow); SA rebuke undead, spells; SQ astrix companion, cold resistance 5, group fighting, +2 bonus on Survival checks in Northlands; AL LE; SV Fort +6, Ref +1, Will +6; Str 16, Dex 10, Con 13, Int 10, Wis 15, Cha 8.

Skills: Concentration +8 (+12), Craft (weaponsmithing) +2, Handle Animal +3, Heal +9, Intimidate +6, Knowledge (Northlands) +2, Knowledge (religion) +3, Profession (soldier) +3, Spellcraft +3.

Feats: Combat Casting, Improved Initiative, Power Attack, Weapon Focus (longsword).

Languages: Black Tongue, Erenlander, Norther, Orcish.

Spells Prepared (5/4+1/3+1; base DC = 12 + spell level; domains: destruction and war): 0—*detect magic, detect poison, guidance, read magic, resistance;* 1st—*bane, cause fear, cure light wounds, magic weapon*, shield of faith;* 2nd—*bull's strength, darkness, shatter, spiritual weapon*.*

* Indicates domain spells.

Possessions: Full plate, large steel shield, master-work longsword, heavy crossbow, 20 bolts, scroll of *cure moderate wounds*, scroll of *sound burst*, scroll of *speak with dead*, fine ceremonial clothing, ornate scroll case, 35 gp, 50 gp worth of fine alcohol, maps, metals, silks, and spices.

Veteran Soldier Legate

Male Dorn Lgt4/Ftr4: CR 8; Medium Humanoid (6 ft. 5 in. tall); HD 4d8+4d10+8; hp 50; Init +4; Spd 20 ft.; AC 21 (+0 Dex, +8 masterwork full plate, +2 masterwork large steel shield); Base Atk +7; Grp +10; Atk +12 melee (1d8+5, masterwork longsword) or +8 ranged (1d8+3, composite longbow [Str 16]); SA rebuke undead, spells; SQ astrix companion, cold resistance 5, group fighting, +2 bonus on Survival checks in Northlands; AL LE; SV Fort +11, Ref +4, Will +8; Str 16, Dex 12, Con 13, Int 10, Wis 15, Cha 8.

Skills: Concentration +8 (+12), Craft (weaponsmithing) +2, Handle Animal +7, Heal +11, Intimidate +6, Knowledge (Northlands) +2, Knowledge (religion) +3, Profession (soldier) +7, Spellcraft +3.

Feats: Cleave, Combat Casting, Improved Initiative, Point Blank Shot, Power Attack, Precise Shot, Weapon Focus (longsword), Weapon Specialization (longsword).

Languages: Black Tongue, Erenlander, Norther, Orcish.

Spells Prepared (5/4+1/3+1; base DC = 13 + spell level; domains: death and war): 0—*detect magic, detect poison, guidance, read magic, resistance;* 1st—*bane, cause fear*, cure light wounds, magic weapon, shield of faith;* 2nd—*bull's strength, darkness, death knell*, spiritual weapon.*

* Indicates domain spells.

Possessions: Masterwork full plate, masterwork large steel shield, masterwork longsword, composite longbow [Str 16], arrows (20), masterwork arrows (20), *+1 flaming arrows (20), cloak of protection +1, potion of levitate, potion of rage,* scroll of *cure serious wounds* (x2), scroll of *dispel magic*, scroll of *speak with dead*, ornate scroll case, 35 gp, 100 gp worth of fine alcohol, maps, metals, and spices.

Temple Legate

Male Sarcosan Lgt8: CR 8; Medium Humanoid (5 ft. 4 in. tall); HD 8d8+8; hp 47; Init –1 (Dex); Spd 20 ft.; AC 15 (–1 Dex, *+1 chain shirt, +1 ring of protection*); Base Atk +6; Grp +6; Atk +7 melee (1d6, masterwork light mace); SA rebuke undead, spells; SQ astrix companion, +1 on weapon damage rolls from horseback, natural horseman, +2 bonus on Survival on southern plains, +2 bonus on Gather Information and Knowledge in large cities; AL LE; SV Fort +7, Ref +2, Will +9; Str 10, Dex 8, Con 12, Int 13, Wis 17, Cha 14.

Skills: Bluff +4, Concentration +8, Diplomacy +11, Intimidate +3, Knowledge (arcana) +3, Knowledge (southern Erenland) +2, Knowledge (religion) +7, Sense Motive +5, Spellcraft +7.

Feats: Scribe Scroll, Skill Focus (Diplomacy), Spell Focus (Necromancy), Spell Focus (Enchantment).

Languages: Black Tongue, Colonial, Courtier, Erenlander, and Trader's Tongue.

Spells Prepared (6/5+1/4+1/4+1/2+1; base DC = 13 + spell level; domains: death and evil): 0—*detect magic, detect poison, guidance, read magic (x2), resistance;* 1st—*bane†, cause fear*†, comprehend languages, cure light wounds, entropic shield, sanctuary;* 2nd—*cure moderate wounds, darkness, desecrate*†, enthrall†, hold person†;* 3rd—*animate dead*†, bestow curse†, blindness/deafness, dispel magic, prayer;* 4th—*discern lies, poison†, unholy blight*.*

* Indicates domain spell.

† Enchantment or Necromancy spell. The base save DC for these spells, where applicable, is 14 + spell level.

Possessions: +1 *chain shirt*, large steel shield, masterwork light mace, +1 *ring of protection, potion of levitate, potion of blur, potion of gaseous form,* scroll of *command,* scroll of *cure moderate wounds,* scroll of *glyph of warding,* scroll of *neutralize poison,* scroll of *restoration,* scroll of *commune,* 40 gp, 150 gp worth of fine alcohol, maps, metals, perfumes, silks, and spices.

Sample Orcs

*Note—all skill totals are calculated with armor check penalties included.

Orc Recruit

Male Orc War1: CR 1; Medium Humanoid; HD 1d8+3; hp 7; Init +1; Spd 20 ft.; AC 16, touch 11, flat-footed 15; Atk +5 melee (1d12+4, vardatch) or +2 ranged (1d6+4, javelin); SQ orc traits; AL CE; SV Fort +5, Ref +1, Will +0; Str 18, Dex 12, Con 16, Int 8, Wis 10, Cha 8.

Skills*: Climb −1, Intimidate +1, Jump −1, Survival +2.

Feats: Power Attack

Languages: Black Tongue, Old Dwarven Pidgin, High Elven Pidgin, Orcish.

Possessions: Scale mail, small wooden shield, vardatch, dagger, javelins (2), 2 man-days of rations.

Orc Trooper

Male Orc Ftr2: CR 2; Medium Humanoid; HD 2d10+6; hp 17; Init +1; Spd 20 ft.; AC 17, touch 11, flat-footed 16; Atk +7 melee (1d12+4, vardatch) or +3 ranged (1d6+4, javelin); SQ orc traits; AL NE; SV Fort +6, Ref +1, Will +0; Str 18, Dex 12, Con 16, Int 8, Wis 10, Cha 8.

Skills: Climb –2, Intimidate +2, Jump –2, Survival +2.

Feats: Power Attack, Cleave, Weapon Focus (vardatch).

Languages & Possessions: Same as orc recruit, plus large steel shield and 2 extra javelins.

Orc Scout

Male Orc Rog1/War2: CR 2; Medium Humanoid; HD 1d6+2d8; hp 12; Init +2; Spd 30 ft.; AC 15, touch 12, flatfooted 13; Atk +4 melee (1d6+2, hand axe) or +4 ranged (1d8, light crossbow); SA sneak attack +1d6; SQ orc traits, trapfinding; AL CE; SV Fort +3, Ref +4, Will +2; Str 14, Dex 14, Con 10, Int 10, Wis 14, Cha 8.

Skills: Climb +6, Handle Animal +2, Hide +6, Intimidate +7, Jump +2, Knowledge (Northern Marches) –1, Listen +6, Move Silently +6, Search +4, Sleight of Hand +4, Spot +6, Use Rope +4, Survival +6.

Feats: Dodge, Track.

Languages: Black Tongue, Old Dwarven Pidgin, High Elven Pidgin, Trader's Tongue, Orcish.

Possessions: Leather armor, small wooden shield, light crossbow, hand axes (2), 3 man-days of rations.

Orc Elite

Male Orc Ftr2/Bar1: CR 3; Medium Humanoid; HD 2d10+1d12+9; hp 24; Init +1; Spd 30 ft.; AC 18, touch 11, flatfooted 16; Atk +8 melee (1d12+4, vardatch) or +4 ranged (1d6+4, javelin); SQ orc traits, fast movement, rage 1/day; AL NE; SV Fort +8, Ref +1, Will +0; Str 18, Dex 12, Con 16, Int 8, Wis 10, Cha 8.

Skills: Climb –1, Intimidate +1, Jump –1, Knowledge (Northern Marches) +2, Survival +2.

Feats: Power Attack, Cleave, Improved Sunder, Weapon Focus (vardatch).

Languages: Black Tongue, Old Dwarven Pidgin, High Elven Pidgin, Orcish.

Possessions: Breastplate, large steel shield, vardatch, dagger, javelins (4), 2 man-days of rations.

Orc Marauder

Male Orc Rog3/Bar5: CR 8; Medium Humanoid; 3d6+5d12+16; 61 hp; Init +4; Spd 40 ft.; AC 15 (+3 Dex, +2 leather); Base Atk +7; Grp +11; Atk: +12/+7 melee (1d12+6, masterwork vardatch, two-handed) or +10/+5 melee (1d12+4, masterwork vardatch) and +10 melee (1d6+2, throwing axe), or +11 ranged (1d6+4, composite shortbow [+4 Str]); SA sneak attack +2d6; SQ orc traits, rage 2/day, evasion, uncanny dodge, trap sense +2, trapfinding, fast movement, improved uncanny dodge; AL CE; SV Fort +7, Ref +7, Will +2; Str 18, Dex 16, Con 14, Int 8, Wis 10, Cha 6.

Skills: Climb +11, Hide +9, Intimidate +4, Listen +7, Move Silently +9, Search +5, Spot +6, Survival +7, Tumble +9.

Feats: Point Blank Shot, Rapid Shot, Two-Weapon Fighting.

Languages: Black Tongue, Old Dwarven Pidgin, High Elven Pidgin, Orcish.

Possessions: Leather armor, masterwork vardatch, throwing axes (3), composite shortbow [+4 Str], arrows (30), orcish plagueskulls (3), *potion of cure moderate wounds* (x2), *elemental gem, elixir of fire breath*, 12 man-days of rations.

Oruk Shock Troop

Male Oruk Ftr1: CR 3; Large Giant (8 ft. 10 in. tall); HD 3d8+1d10+12; hp 31; Init +1; Spd 20 ft.; AC 16 (–1 size, +7 half plate); Base Atk +3; Grp +13; Atk +9 melee (3d6+7, large greataxe) or +3 ranged (1d8+5, large javelin); Space/Reach 10 ft./10 ft.; SQ light sensitivity, orc/ogre blood; AL LE; SV Fort +8, Ref +1, Will +2; Str 21, Dex 11, Con 16, Int 10, Wis 10, Cha 4.

Skills: Climb +2, Jump +2, Listen +3, Spot +3.

Feats: Cleave, Power Attack, Weapon Focus (greataxe).

Languages: Black Tongue, Orcish.

Possessions: Half plate, large greataxe, large javelins (3), 4 man-days rations, 10 gp worth of alcohol, cured meats, and salt.

Oruk Commander

Male Oruk Ftr6: CR 8; Large Giant (9 ft. 4 in. tall); HD 3d8+6d10+27; hp 73; Init +1; Spd 20 ft.; AC 20 (–1 size, +1 Dex, +8 masterwork full plate, +2 large steel shield); Base Atk +8; Grp +17; Atk +15/+10 melee (2d6+8, masterwork greater crafted vardatch) or +10/+5 ranged (1d8+4, masterwork composite longbow [Str 18]); Space/Reach 10 ft./10 ft.; SQ light sensitivity, orc/ogre blood; AL LE; SV Fort +11, Ref +4, Will +4; Str 22, Dex 12, Con 16, Int 10, Wis 13, Cha 9.

Skills: Climb +7, Jump +7, Listen +3, Spot +3.

Feats: Cleave, Great Cleave, Improved Bull Rush, Improved Sunder, Power Attack, Weapon Focus (vardatch), Weapon Specialization (vardatch).

Languages: Black Tongue, Norther, Orcish.

Possessions: masterwork full plate, large steel shield, masterwork vardatch, masterwork composite longbow [+4 Str], arrows (20), *+1 flaming arrows* (5), *+1 seeking arrows* (5), *potion of cure serious wounds*, 4 man-days rations, 50 gp worth of alcohol, cured meats, maps, metals, and salt.

Appendix 1: D&D 3.5 Updated Midnight Spell List

Abjuration

0-Level Spells
Resistance

1st-Level Spells
Alarm
Endure Elements
Hold Portal
Hide from Animals
Protection from Chaos
Protection from Evil
Protection from Good
Protection from Law
Shield
Undetectable Alignment

2nd-Level Spells
Arcane Lock
Obscure Object
Protection from Arrows
Resist Energy

3rd-Level Spells
Dispel Magic
Explosive Runes
Magic Circle Against Chaos
Magic Circle Against Evil
Magic Circle Against Good
Magic Circle Against Law
Nondetection
Protection from Energy

4th-Level Spells
Antiplant Shell
Dimensional Anchor
Fire Trap
Freedom of Movement
Globe of Invulnerability,
   Lesser
Remove Curse
Repel Vermin
Stoneskin

5th-Level Spells
Atonement
Break Enchantment
Private Sanctum

6th-Level Spells
Antilife Shell
Antimagic Field
Dispel Magic, Greater
Globe of Invulnerability
Guards and Wards
Repulsion

7th-Level Spells
Sequester
Spell Turning

8th-Level Spells
Dimensional Lock
Mind Blank
Prismatic Wall
Protection from Spells
Repel Metal or Stone

9th-Level Spells
Antipathy
Freedom
Imprisonment
Disjunction
Prismatic Sphere

Conjuration, Greater

0-Level Spells
Summon Instrument

1st-Level Spells
Mount
Summon Monster I
Summon Nature's Ally I

2nd-Level Spells
Summon Monster II
Summon Nature's Ally II
Summon Swarm

3rd-Level Spells
Summon Monster III
Summon Nature's Ally III

4th-Level Spells
Summon Monster IV
Summon Nature's Ally IV

5th-Level Spells
Insect Plague
Summon Monster V
Summon Nature's Ally V

6th-Level Spells
Summon Monster VI
Summon Nature's Ally VI

7th-Level Spells
Creeping Doom
Instant Summons
Summon Monster VII
Summon Nature's Ally VII

8th-Level Spells
Summon Monster VIII
Summon Nature's Ally VIII
Trap the Soul

9th-Level Spells
Elemental Swarm
Gate
Storm of Vengeance
Summon Monster IX
Summon Nature's Ally IX

Conjuration, Lesser

0-Level Spells
Acid Splash
Create Water
Cure Minor Wounds

1st-Level Spells
Cure Light Wounds
Grease

Mage Armor
Obscuring Mist
Unseen Servant

2nd-Level Spells
Acid Arrow
Cure Moderate Wounds
Delay Poison
Fog Cloud
Glitterdust
Restoration, Lesser
Web

3rd-Level Spells
Cure Serious Wounds
Neutralize Poison
Phantom Steed
Sepia Snake Sigil
Silver Wind*
Sleet Storm
Stinking Cloud
Remove Disease

4th-Level Spells
Black Tentacles
Cure Critical Wounds
Minor Creation
Secure Shelter
Solid Fog

5th-Level Spells
Cloudkill
Cure Light Wounds, Mass
Faithful Hound
Major Creation
Wall of Stone
Wall of Thorns

6th-Level Spells
Acid Fog
Cure Moderate Wounds,
   Mass
Fire Seeds
Wall of Iron

7th-Level Spells
Heal
Magnificent Mansion
Phase Door
Regenerate

8th-Level Spells
Cure Serious Wounds, Mass
Incendiary Cloud
Trap the Soul

9th-Level Spells
Cure Critical Wounds, Mass
Refuge
Shambler

Divination

0-Level Spells
Detect Magic
Detect Poison
Guidance
Know Direction

Read Magic

1st-Level Spells
Comprehend Languages
Detect Animals or Plants
Detect Astirax*
Detect Secret Doors
Detect Snares and Pits
Detect Undead
Identify
Far Whisper
Speak with Animals
True Strike

2nd-Level Spells
Detect Chaos
Detect Evil
Detect Good
Detect Law
Detect Thoughts
Locate Object
See Invisibility
Tongues

3rd-Level Spells
Arcane Sight
Clairaudience/Clairvoyance
Speak with Plants

4th-Level Spells
Arcane Eye
Detect Scrying
Locate Creature
Scrying

5th-Level Spells
Commune with Nature
Prying Eyes
Telepathic Bond

6th-Level Spells
Analyze Dweomer
Find the Path
Legend Lore
Stone Tell
True Seeing

7th-Level Spells
Arcane Sight, Greater
Scrying, Greater
Vision

8th-Level Spells
Discern Location
Moment of Prescience
Prying Eyes, Greater

9th-Level Spells
Foresight

Enchantment

0-Level Spells
Daze
Lullaby

1st-Level Spells
Calm Animals

Charm Animal
Charm Person
Hypnotism
Confusion, Lesser
Sleep

2nd-Level Spells
Animal Messenger
Animal Trance
Calm Emotions
Daze Monster
Enthrall
Hold Animal
Hideous Laughter
Hypnotic Pattern
Touch of Idiocy

3rd-Level Spells
Deep Slumber
Dominate Animal
Heroism
Hold Person
Rage
Suggestion

4th-Level Spells
Charm Monster
Confusion
Crushing Despair
Geas, Lesser
Modify Memory

5th-Level Spells
Dominate Person
Feeblemind
Hold Monster
Mind Fog
Symbol of Sleep
Song of Discord

6th-Level Spells
Geas/Quest
Heroism, Greater
Suggestion, Mass
Symbol of Persuasion

7th-Level Spells
Hold Person, Mass
Insanity
Power Word Blind
Symbol of Stunning

8th-Level Spells
Antipathy
Binding
Charm Monster, Mass
Command Plants
Demand
Irresistable Dance
Power Word Stun
Symbol of Insanity
Sympathy

9th-Level Spells
Dominate Monster
Hold Monster, Mass
Power Word Kill

Evocation, Greater

0-Level Spells
Ray of Frost

1st-Level Spells
Burning Hands
Floating Disk
Magic Missile
Shocking Grasp

2nd-Level Spells
Continual Flame
Flame Blade
Flaming Sphere
Gust of Wind
Produce Flame
Scorching Ray

3rd-Level Spells
Call Lightning
Fireball
Tiny Hut
Lightning Bolt
Wind Wall

4th-Level Spells
Fire Shield
Flame Strike
Ice Storm
Resilent Sphere
Wall of Fire
Wall of Ice

5th-Level Spells
Call Lightning Storm
Cone of Cold
Hallow
Unhallow
Wall of Force

6th-Level Spells
Chain Lightning
Freezing Sphere

7th-Level Spells
Delayed Blast Fireball
Fire Storm
Forcecage
Sword

8th-Level Spells
Polar Ray
Telekinetic Sphere
Whirlwind

9th-Level Spells
Meteor Swarm

Evocation, Lesser

0-Level Spells
Dancing Lights
Flare
Light

1st-Level Spells
Faerie Fire

2nd-Level Spells
Darkness
Daylight

Shatter
Sound Burst

4th-Level Spells
Shout

5th-Level Spells
Hallow
Interposing Hand
Sending
Unhallow

6th-Level Spells
Forceful Hand
Contingency

7th-Level Spells
Grasping Hand
Prismatic Spray
Sunbeam

8th-Level Spells
Clenched Fist
Earthquake
Shout, Greater
Sunburst

9th-Level Spells
Crushing Hand

Illusion

0-Level Spells
Dancing Lights
Ghost Sound

1st-level Spells
Color Spray
Disguise Self
Disguise Weapon*
Magic Aura
Silent Image
Undetectable Aura
Ventriloquism

2nd-level Spells
Blur
Disguise Ally*
Greenshield*
Hypnotic Pattern
Invisibility
Magic Mouth
Minor Image
Mirror Image
Misdirection
Silence
Trap

3rd-level Spells
Cover the Scent
Displacement
Illusory Script
Invisibility Sphere
Major Image

4th-level Spells
Hallucinatory Terrain
Illusory Wall
Invisibility, Greater
Phantasmal Killer
Rainbow Pattern

Shadow Conjuration

5th-level Spells
Dream
False Vision
Mirage Arcana
Nightmare
Persistent Image
Seeming
Shadow Evocation

6th-level Spells
Mislead
Permanent Image
Programmed Image
Shadow Walk
Veil

7th-level Spells
Invisibility, Mass
Project Image
Shadow Conjuration, Greater
Simulacrum

8th-level Spells
Scintillating Pattern
Screen
Shadow Evocation, Greater

9th-level Spells
Shades
Weird

Necromancy

0-Level Spells
Disrupt Undead
Touch of Fatigue

1st-level spells
Cause Fear
Chill Touch
Ray of Enfeeblement

2nd-level spells
Blindness/Deafness
Command Undead
False Life
Ghoul Touch
Scare
Spectral Hand

3rd-level spells
Gentle Repose
Halt Undead
Poison
Ray of Exhaustion
Vampiric Touch

4th-level spells
Animate Dead
Bestow Curse
Contagion
Enervation
Fear

5th-level spells
Blight
Death Ward
Magic Jar

Nexus Fuel*
Symbol of Pain
Waves of Fatigue

6th-level spells
Circle of Death
Create Undead
Eyebite
Symbol of Fear
Undeath to Death

7th-level spells
Control Undead
Finger of Death
Symbol of Weakness
Waves of Exhaustion

8th-level spells
Clone
Create Greater Undead
Horrid Wilting
Symbol of Death

9th-level spells
Energy Drain
Soul Bind
Wail of the Banshee

Transmutation

0-Level Spells

Mage Hand
Mending
Open/Close
Virtue

1st-level spells
Animate Rope
Enlarge Person
Entangle
Erase
Feather Fall
Goodberry
Jump
Longstrider
Magic Fang
Magic Stone
Magic Weapon
Pass Without Trace
Reduce Person
Shillelagh
Stone Soup*

2nd-level spells
Alter Self
Barkskin
Bear's Endurance
Bull's Strength
Cat's Grace
Chill Metal
Darkvision
Eagle's Splendor
Fox's Cunning
Heat Metal
Knock
Levitate
Lifetrap*
Nature's Revelation*
Owl's Wisdom
Pyrotechnics
Rope Trick

Silver Blood*
Soften Earth and Stone
Spider Climb
Tree Shape
Warp Wood
Whispering Wind
Wood Shape

3rd-level spells
Charm Repair*
Diminish Plants
Flame Arrow
Fly
Gaseous Form
Halfling Burrow*
Haste
Magic Fang, Greater
Magic Weapon, Greater
Keen Edge
Meld into Stone
Plant Growth
Quench
Secret Page
Shrink Item
Slow
Snare
Spike Growth
Water Breathing
Water Walk

4th-level spells
Air Walk
Enlarge Person, Mass
Giant Vermin
Polymorph
Polymorph Self
Mnemonic Enhancer
Reduce Person, Mass
Reincarnate
Rusting Grasp
Silver Storm*
Spike Stones
Stone Shape

5th-level spells
Animal Growth
Awaken
Baleful Polymorph
Control Winds
Fabricate
Overland Flight
Passwall
Telekinesis
Transmute Mud to Rock
Transmute Rock to Mud

6th-level spells
Bear's Endurance, Mass
Bull's Strength, Mass
Cat's Grace, Mass
Control Water
Disintegrate
Eagle's Splendor, Mass
Flesh to Stone
Fox's Cunning, Mass
Ironwood
Liveoak
Lucubration
Move Earth
Owl's Wisdom, Mass
Repel Wood

Spellstaff
Stone to Flesh
Transformation
Wind Walk

7th-level spells
Changestaff
Control Weather
Reverse Gravity
Statue
Transmute Metal to Wood
Whirlwind

8th-level
Animal Shapes
Control Plants
Iron Body
Polymorph Any Object
Temporal Stasis

9th-level
Shapechange
Time Stop

Universal

0-Level Spells
Arcane Mark
Prestidigitation

5th-Level Spells
Permanency

7th-Level Spells
Limited Wish

9th-Level Spell
Wish

* Described in MIDNIGHT: Against the Shadow

Appendix 2:

Errata for Midnight (MN) and MIDNIGHT: Against the Shadow (AgS).

MN—Every class in Midnight receives Profession as a class skill.

MN—Icewood bows: Icewood bows do not have unique stats or qualities other than that they may be enchanted using one-half the standard resources of time, components, and energy. These bows tend to be masterwork.

MN p. 30—Orcs receive a +1 bonus on damage rolls vs. dwarves, rather than a +1 bonus on attack rolls vs. dwarves.

MN p. 36—A 2nd-level channeler/1st-level rogue can only cast 2nd-level spells, not 3rd-level spells.

MN p. 36—Characters with more channeler levels than levels in other classes add +1 to their character levels *only* for determining the highest level spells they can cast, but not for other purposes, like caster level of spells.

MN p. 40—Precise Strike should read "For every 6 levels of defender the character has, he ignores one point of armor bonus to AC. Also, at 6th level his strikes count as magic weapons for overcoming damage reduction, at 12th level they count as alignment weapons (as per the defend-

er's alignment) for overcoming damage reduction, and at 18th level they count as adamantium for overcoming damage reduction.

MN p. 68—Strategic Blow should read "Starting at 2nd level." Also, change the DR bypass as follows: silver instead of +1, magic instead of +2, cold iron instead of +3, alignment instead of +4, and adamantine instead of +5.

MN p. 71—Under the Magecraft feat, add to the end of the Benefit section: "The caster level for a character using this feat to cast spells is equal to his character level."

MN p. 71—Sarcosan pureblood prerequisite: Must be a Sarcosan.

MN p. 251—Add *Purify Food and Drink* to the channeler spell list.

AgS p. 31—Pureblood heroic path prerequisite: Must be an Erenlander

AtS p. 35—Unstoppable Voice should read "Beginning at 11th level" and Control Power Word should read "Upon reaching 17th level."

AtS p. 38—Tactitian gains Coordinated Attack 2/day at 8th level, 3/day at 12th level, and 4/day at 17th level.